"To anyone familiar with recent initiatives in Protestant life and thought, it is no surprise that Allen and Swain would coauthor such a stirring summons to embrace the fullness of historic Christian catholicity. What many will find surprising is that their 'renewal through retrieval' manifesto takes the form of rehabilitating the much-abused doctrine of *sola Scriptura*, by turns defending it from detractors and rescuing it from misguided champions. In their hands, this venerable doctrine resumes its function as a guide for engaging the riches of the church's historic confession, not as an excuse for ignoring pre-Reformation exegesis. Here is Protestant theology that understands itself, its source, and its context with refreshing clarity."

—Fred Sanders, Torrey Honors Institute, Biola University

"*Reformed Catholicity* is a timely and important book. While slim in size, it is weighty in its message, which not only encourages us to recognize how we are all 'traditioned' in our faith but also invites us to enter this lively stream that flows from the Scriptures through the people of God to us. Thankfully, these wise authors avoid the growing forms of naive primitivism becoming popular in some circles while also steering clear of the sectarian theological isolation proposed by others. Instead, they invite readers to embrace Reformed catholicity, a theologically informed approach that humbly responds to the revelation of the Triune God, recognizing the organic connection between Scripture and dogma, consciously drawing upon and in conversation with the wisdom of the historic church in both her universal and particular expressions."

—Kelly M. Kapic, Covenant College

"A refreshing and encouraging retrieval of the church's rich tradition is occurring among evangelicals in a manner and depth that would have been well-nigh unimaginable thirty years ago. *Reformed Catholicity* admirably reflects this engagement and will help Reformed readers— and those from other traditions—to embrace ever more deeply the wonder and glory of the blessed Trinity."

—Christopher A. Hall, Eastern University

REFORMED CATHOLICITY

The Promise of Retrieval for Theology
and Biblical Interpretation

MICHAEL ALLEN
AND SCOTT R. SWAIN

AFTERWORD BY J. TODD BILLINGS

BakerAcademic
a division of Baker Publishing Group
Grand Rapids, Michigan

Published by Baker Academic
a division of Baker Publishing Group
PO Box 6287, Grand Rapids, MI 49516-6287
www.bakeracademic.com

Printed in the United States of America

Library of Congress Cataloging-in-Publication Data
Allen, Michael, 1981–
    Reformed catholicity : the promise of retrieval for theology and biblical inter-
pretation / Michael Allen and Scott R. Swain. — 3.
        pages cm
    Includes bibliographical references and index.
    ISBN 978-0-8010-4979-8 (pbk.)
        1. Theology. 2. Bible—Criticism, interpretation, etc. 3. Church renewal. I. Title.
BR118.A435 2015
230—dc23   2014028821

Baker Publishing Group publications use paper produced from sustainable forestry practices and post-consumer waste whenever possible.

Contents

Acknowledgments

We rejoice in the fact that this book is not suggesting a new path but is offering analysis of what we see occurring around us already. So we give thanks for friends and exemplars of Reformed catholicity and of renewal through retrieval. We are delighted to be involved in a number of projects that exemplify, in many ways, the project of Reformed catholicity: specifically, Baker Academic's *Christian Dogmatics* project and Zondervan Academic's New Studies in Dogmatics series. We realized, amid these varying ongoing involvements, that it was time to step back and speak programmatically about what such projects assume, namely, a passionate commitment of many to do theology in the context of the catholic and Reformed church. We think there is a serious need for a dogmatic proposal as to why these various recent movements are to be encouraged and how they can best be furthered. We hope that this manifesto does not conclude a conversation, by any means, but acknowledges the progress of developments already taking place and offers some analytical clarity regarding this newfound commitment to a Reformed-catholic *ressourcement* for the sake of mission and renewal.

We should note those who were willing to read the manuscript (or portions thereof) and offer feedback: John Webster, Todd Billings, Paul Nimmo, Wesley Hill, Jono Linebaugh, Dan Treier, and Kevin Vanhoozer. Their keen eyes and insightful suggestions have reformed the book, no doubt, and any remaining errors are borne by the authors alone. And, of course, we are most delighted that Todd Billings was willing to write the afterword. Todd is an astute historian and as talented a theologian as one will find anywhere. Most importantly, for him those two callings are not separated. Indeed, he embodies the persona of a Reformed catholic, and we are honored that his own proposal concludes this volume and relates it to the life and ministry of local congregations.

We thank our wives, Emily and Leigh, as well as our children for their support in the preparation of this book. We also thank our respective institutions for supporting our research and writing; in particular, Luder Whitlock and Don Sweeting deserve thanks for protecting our time and encouraging this work. The team at Baker Academic has proven remarkable in moving this volume to press with speed and skill; we are thankful for Bob Hosack, Robert Hand, Bryan Dyer, Mason Slater, Jeremy Wells, and Trinity Graeser.

We dedicate this book to Professor John Webster, now of the University of St. Andrews. John has been many things to us: examiner, editor, colleague, and friend. Beyond these various institutional and personal roles, however, he has been a mentor to so many younger theologians in the catholic and Reformed world today. His writings and his institutional service have helped shape a context where Reformed catholicity is a reality and, we believe, one with strong intellectual vitality. For his leadership, example, friendship, and faithfulness, we are most grateful.

Introduction

Renewal through Retrieval

Can Christians and churches be catholic and Reformed? Can they commit themselves not only to the ultimate authority of apostolic Scripture but also to receiving this Bible within the context of the apostolic church?

> There is no other such gulf in the history of human thought as that which is cleft between the apostolic and the immediately succeeding ages. To pass from the latest apostolic writings to the earliest compositions of uninspired Christian pens is to fall through such a giddy height that it is no wonder if we rise dazed and almost unable to determine our whereabouts. Here is the great fault—as the geologists would say—in the history of Christian doctrine. There is every evidence of continuity—but, oh, at how much lower a level! The rich vein of evangelical religion has run well-nigh out; and, though there are masses of apostolic origin lying everywhere, they are but fragments, and are evidently only the talus which has fallen from the cliffs above and scattered itself over the lower surface.[1]

1. B. B. Warfield, *The Significance of the Westminster Standards as a Creed* (New York: Charles Scribner's Sons, 1898), 4.

1

With these pointed words, B. B. Warfield critiques the theology of the post-apostolic church for falling short of the perfections of the writings of the prophets and apostles.[2] The stalwart defender of Reformed Orthodoxy at Princeton Theological Seminary offers a value judgment about not only the biblical writings and their relevance today, but also (by comparison) the post-apostolic witness of the early church. In such a vision, of course, to be Reformed means precisely to cease being catholic or, at the very least, to limit the extent of the catholic tradition that is valid and authentic. Thankfully, Warfield's wider reflections do not demonstrate a consistency in this regard, and he was surely no thoroughgoing iconoclast with respect to the patristic and medieval heritage of the Reformational church; yet his reflections here on the collapse of the catholic faith have resonated through much of the evangelical and Reformed world. Indeed,

2. Charles Hodge had earlier offered both a more subtle approach to the catholic heritage of the church as well as some specific language that was rhetorically unfortunate (see Charles Hodge, *Systematic Theology*, vol. 1, *Theology* [Grand Rapids: Eerdmans, 1970]). In the midst of a sober reflection on the development of doctrine (116–18) Hodge affirms that doctrine does develop, and that this extension of biblical teaching is a positive sign and instrument in the formation of Christians and churches. Later he polemically engages what he terms "Romish" developments in faith and practice and, more broadly, the Roman Catholic doctrine of tradition (see 121, where this is the explicit concern). In the course of those polemics, he sometimes speaks more unguardedly of tradition itself as a detriment:

> Tradition teaches error, and therefore cannot be divinely controlled so as to be a rule of faith. The issue is between Scripture and tradition. Both cannot be true. The one contradicts the other. One or the other must be given up. Of this at least no true Protestant has any doubt. All the doctrines peculiar to Romanism, and for which Romanists plead the authority of Scripture, Protestants believe to be anti-scriptural; and therefore they need no other evidence to prove that tradition is not to be trusted either in matters of faith and practice. (128–29)

If one reads Hodge contextually, it is clear that he is opposing the Roman Catholic doctrine of tradition, which he has earlier characterized as a view that tradition is a "second source" of independent and "equal authority" to the Scriptures (earlier on 128). Admittedly, however, his rhetoric here can sound much more all-encompassing, and we do well to be cognizant of the danger that he might be easily misread (either by those who would do so to condemn him or to herald what they believe he says). A much more effective account of tradition from the Princeton theologians is offered by Warfield's successor, who maintains the same principled approach but does so without any of the ambiguous rhetoric: see John Murray, "Tradition: Romish and Protestant," in *Collected Writings of John Murray*, vol. 4, *Studies in Theology* (Edinburgh: Banner of Truth, 1982), 264–73, esp. 268–69.

anything after the apostolic age would be a distraction to many. The call, then, is for reform by return to primitivism, peeling back layers of ecclesial development and getting to the canonical core.[3]

Many critiques of Protestantism suggest that if one desires a churchly, sacramental, ancient faith, then one must turn from the Reformation toward Rome or the East. And many have taken to those paths, fleeing what they may perceive to be thin theologies of ministry and of the Christian life in the Reformational world. Others celebrate the Reformed church as decidedly un-catholic and seek to minimize any connection to the ancient shape of the Christian faith. Whether fleeing or staying, such postures derive from a view of theology and history, namely, how one believes Reformed Christians view the catholic heritage of the Christian church. Such postures fit with the assessment of Warfield, as seen above, and their fervor has only increased in more recent decades.

But there is another way, which predates the historical assessment of Warfield. William Perkins, the great source of so much Reformed piety in the Puritan era, penned a treatise entitled *Reformed Catholicke* to make the point that Reformed identity was precisely a matter of Reformed catholicity. Perkins was Reformed, a Puritan even, but he believed that efforts to see the church purified and reformed did not remove its liturgy, its instruments for discipleship, or its approaches to government; rather such efforts refined them. "By a Reformed Catholic, I understand anyone that holds the same necessary heads of religion with the Roman Church: yet so as he pares off and rejects all errors in doctrine, whereby the said religion is corrupted."[4] Perkins teases out this common catholic heritage and cherished tradition with respect to two things: faith and practice. Respecting faith, he later says: "And many things we hold for truth, not written in the word, if they be not against the word."[5] Concerning practice, he writes: "We hold that the Church of God hath power to prescribe ordinances,

---

3. The frequent language employed by N. T. Wright to refuse to let the Jesus of the creeds get in the way of the Jesus of the gospel is a prime example (see *How God Became King: The Forgotten Story of the Gospels* [New York: HarperOne, 2012] as a recent example of this recurring theme in his work).

4. William Perkins, *A Reformed Catholicke*, Works of William Perkins 1 (London: John Legatt, 1626), 555.

5. Ibid., 580.

rules, or traditions, touching time and place of God's worship, and touching order and comeliness in the same. . . . This kind of tradition, whether made by general Councils or particular Synods, we have care to maintain and observe."[6] In this book our wager is that Perkins was right: to be Reformed means to go deeper into true catholicity, not to move away from catholicity.

Recent Trends in Faith and Practice

A number of theological trends have arisen in recent decades, each of which celebrates or calls for retrieving elements, practices, and texts from earlier Christian churches. Our call toward Reformed catholicity is not that of a lone voice calling in the wilderness. As we will see in our survey, these movements vary quite a bit and even disagree on a host of issues. In our judgment, they also exhibit varying degrees of historical and theological perception and discrimination. They coalesce, however, in the judgment that modern theology, in more conservative and pro-gressive forms, has exhausted itself as a mode of theological inquiry and that the path toward theological renewal lies in retrieving resources from the Christian tradition. We will offer the briefest of surveys.

Nouvelle Théologie

The first notable movement toward retrieval was led by a number of Roman Catholic theologians, Yves Congar and Henri de Lubac being the most notable. What became known as "the new theology" (*la nouvelle théologie*) was, perhaps ironically, largely characterized by an attempt to recover the riches of patristic theology for the sake of engaging the modern world more effectively. Initially these theo-logians were marginalized and even disciplined by their superiors; eventually, however, their influence shaped Vatican II and more recent Roman Catholic developments, in particular the pontificates of John Paul II and Benedict XVI.[7]

---

6. Ibid., 581.
7. For analysis of the most significant of these theologians (as well as a few others), see Fergus Kerr, *Twentieth Century Catholic Theologians: From Neo-Scholasticism to Nuptial Mystery* (Oxford: Blackwell, 2006).

Karl Barth and the Revival of Dogmatic Theology

At roughly the same time, Karl Barth worked—seemingly alone—to turn the scene of academic theology in Germany and Switzerland back to the classical sources of Christian faith and practice. While Barth is sometimes identified as a member of the "dialectical theology" movement or of "neo-orthodoxy" (along with Rudolf Bultmann, Emil Brunner, or Paul Tillich), there are sizable differences between these figures, and it is worthwhile to consider Barth as distinct from these other figures. In terms of ongoing significance, it was Barth's writings (both in his voluminous *Church Dogmatics* and in his published lectures) that reintroduced modern theological students to sources from the classical and Reformational tradition. Barth obviously did his work mindful of the various epistemological and metaphysical challenges of the modern era, but his working approach was by way of resourcing theologians with traditional tools to aid in testifying to the gospel faithfully.

Reception History (Wirkungsgeschichte) of the Bible

In the last few years there has been a rising swell of interest in what is often referred to as the reception history of biblical texts. The biblical studies guild has focused largely in recent decades upon historical readings of scriptural texts; reception history remains a historical discipline—in this case, however, focused upon the aftereffects, or reception, of a text rather than the precursors to or background of a text. Among many practitioners, it also remains a largely descriptive, nonevaluative discipline that prescinds from making judgments about the propriety or impropriety of various traditions of biblical reception. Two commentary series illustrate this movement: the Blackwell Bible Commentary and the newly released Illuminations commentary series. Further, a number of monographs, collections of essays, and conferences have focused upon how various figures, churches, or movements have read specific texts.

Donald Bloesch and "Consensual Christianity"

Donald Bloesch, the late United Church of Christ theologian, addressed the Protestant mainline church with the promise of what he called "consensual Christianity." Bloesch published a multivolume systematic theology entitled "Christian Foundations," and the title is meant to connote the basic firmament of Christian faith and practice, derived from Holy Scripture and developed in the course of the church's witness. In a context where the Protestant mainline church was pulled in directions of revision and pluralism, Bloesch spent his career pointing to the apostolic gospel and the deep consensus of Christians across the centuries and over denominational divides regarding its nature and implications.

Thomas Oden's "Paleo-Orthodoxy"

A contemporary of Bloesch, Thomas Oden, experienced a major shift during his academic career from a commitment to liberal Protestantism to a deep devotion to what he referred to as "paleo-orthodoxy." Oden taught systematic theology in a Methodist context, and his own published theology is best received primarily as a pastiche of patristic theology, a demonstration of the "consensual tradition" that he argues underlies seemingly divergent denominational traditions and stems from the roots of patristic theology, exegesis, and, ultimately, worship. Oden's most significant contribution, however, was his editing the influential series the Ancient Christian Commentary on Scripture (InterVarsity Press). This series covers the entire Bible and provides paragraph-length excerpts from a smattering of patristic sources on every verse, allowing pastors or students to familiarize themselves with some of the exegetical and theological reflections of early Christian fathers. More recently, the publisher has released parallel series that provide excerpts on various topics (Ancient Christian Doctrines) or make accessible new translations of ancient commentaries (Ancient Christian Texts).

Robert Webber's Ancient-Future Christianity

Robert Webber, longtime professor of theology at Wheaton College and then professor of ministry at Northern Seminary, launched a ministry movement known as the ancient-future movement. In the 1970s Webber had begun to speak of *Common Roots* and the need for evangelicals to draw from the Christian past, and he then followed that notable book in the 1980s with *Evangelicals on the Canterbury Trail*.[8] Over the years to come, he developed a worship institute and a series of books that sought to provide biblical teaching on worship, discipleship, and ministry and did so by drawing upon the patristic heritage of the church for the sake of engaging postmodern culture in a profound way. For example, Webber argued that evangelicals would do well to rethink the spiritual significance of time for the sake of discipling Christ-followers in the postmodern era.[9] The Webber Institute for Worship Studies continues to educate pastors and laypeople in these principles, and other institutions have adopted similar approaches (for example, Trinity School for Ministry in Ambridge, Pennsylvania, hosts the Robert E. Webber Center).

The Modern Hymns Movement

A contemporaneous movement, especially in Reformed and Presbyterian churches, has been dubbed the "modern hymns movement." This development, spearheaded by groups like Reformed University Fellowship, Indelible Grace, and Keith and Kristyn Getty, has recast traditional hymns from the church's history into new arrangements that are more modern and very easily sung by a congregation.

Carl Braaten and Robert Jenson's Evangelical Catholicism

Carl Braaten and Robert Jenson both taught within seminaries and colleges in the mainline Lutheran world. They were founding editors of the journal *Dialog*, which introduced modern theological debates into the American Lutheran context in the 1960s. Twenty years later, however, they shifted their focus from calling the church into conversation with recent debates to focusing the church on the classical resources of the ecumenical tradition. They launched the Center for Catholic and Evangelical Theology, began a new journal *Pro Ecclesia*, hosted a number of conferences, and published many

8. Robert E. Webber, *Common Roots: A Call to Evangelical Maturity* (Grand Rapids: Zondervan, 1978); Robert E. Webber, *Evangelicals on the Canterbury Trail* (Waco: Word, 1985).

9. Robert E. Webber, *Ancient-Future Time: Forming Spirituality through the Christian Year* (Grand Rapids: Baker Books, 2004).

books that sought to further ecumenical activity and, to that end, conversation across and through the tradition. For example, one of their most significant edited collections of essays was *The Catholicity of the Reformation*.[10] Engagement of the past was no promise of continued reaffirmation of every facet: Jenson's own systematic theology is revisionary in many ways (especially regarding the doctrine of God's triune being). While Oden and Bloesch may have argued that engagement of the classical tradition led to a continued reaffirmation of what has been called classical theism, others like Robert Webber and Robert Jenson have argued that key elements of that theological heritage require revision in light of scriptural testimony. A shared commitment to retrieval and engagement of the past clearly does not foreclose discussion about how best to proceed.

Theological Interpretation of Scripture

One of the most frequently discussed movements in contemporary theology goes by the names of "theological interpretation of Scripture," "theological exegesis," or "theological commentary." There are various facets to such hermeneutical approaches, but they all include a renewed appreciation for reading the Bible within the context of the catholic church.[11] A number of commentary series in this vein have launched or will soon launch, including the Brazos Theological Commentary on the Bible, the Two Horizons Commentary, and the T&T Clark International Theological Commentary. Monograph series, a journal (the *Journal of Theological Interpretation*), degree programs, and conferences have also been offered regarding theological interpretation. A major focus of this movement is retrieval of premodern modes of scriptural reasoning, suggesting that figural

10. Carl Braaten and Robert Jenson, eds., *The Catholicity of the Reformation* (Grand Rapids: Eerdmans, 1996).

11. See Daniel J. Treier, *Introducing Theological Interpretation of Scripture: Recovering a Christian Practice* (Grand Rapids: Baker Academic, 2008), esp. chaps. 1–3; J. Todd Billings, *The Word of God for the People of God* (Grand Rapids: Eerdmans, 2010), chaps. 1–5; and Scott R. Swain, *Trinity, Revelation, and Reading: A Theological Introduction to the Bible and Its Interpretation* (London: T&T Clark, 2011), chaps. 4–5.

and spiritual hermeneutics as well as the creedally disciplined approach of the early church fathers has something to teach us today.[12]

Radical Orthodoxy

In the 1990s a group of theologians in the United Kingdom, largely in Cambridge, began work on rethinking the place of the church in the modern world. To combat the marginalization of theology, as they saw it, John Milbank and others offered a genealogy of decline: an account of how moves in philosophical theology from the late medieval through the early modern period led to the sociological diminution of theology. Milbank's tome *Theology and Social Theory* was crucial in putting forward this account, and the team-written collection *Radical Orthodoxy* followed a few years later with an account of how this genealogy of decline explained ills in various areas of thought (ranging from aesthetics to economics).[13] A book series followed, and a Center for Theology and Philosophy was launched at the University of Nottingham. In its own way, Radical Orthodoxy sought to explain the decline of the church and to provide a counternarrative by drawing on the heritage of Christian Platonism (which involved readings of Augustine, Aquinas, and others). The nature of historical retrieval offered by those within the Radical Orthodoxy movement has been quite controversial on historical grounds, but the vigor of those debates only manifests how significant historical retrieval is to the Radical Orthodoxy project (whether accurate or not).[14]

12. On retrieving patristic hermeneutics, see John J. O'Keefe and R. R. Reno, *Sanctified Vision: An Introduction to Early Christian Interpretation of the Bible* (Baltimore: Johns Hopkins University Press, 2005); on the benefit of creedally disciplined readings of the Bible, see David S. Yeago, "The New Testament and the Nicene Dogma: A Contribution to the Recovery of Theological Exegesis," *Pro Ecclesia* 3 (1994): 152–64.

13. John Milbank, *Theology and Social Theory* (Oxford: Blackwell, 1993); John Milbank, Catherine Pickstock, and Graham Ward, eds., *Radical Orthodoxy: A New Theology* (London: Routledge, 1998). For brief analysis, see Michael Allen, "Putting Suspenders on the World: Radical Orthodoxy as a Postsecular Theological Proposal or What Can Evangelicals Learn from Postmodern Christian Platonists?" *Themelios* 31, no. 2 (January 2006): 40–53.

14. See, for example, Paul DeHart, *Aquinas and Radical Orthodoxy: A Critical Inquiry* (London: Routledge, 2011).

Evangelical Ressourcement

In recent years a number of evangelical theologians from the Free Church and Reformed traditions have called for a *ressourcement* that draws from the ancient and medieval heritage of the church. D. H. Williams teaches patristics at Baylor University, and he has launched the Evangelical *Ressourcement* series. His own writings argue that evangelical theology needs to look back past the Reformation to the consensus of the early church.[15] Indeed, Williams specifically uses the language of retrieval and renewal in his call for engaging the past for the sake of theology's future.[16] More recently Hans Boersma, a Reformed theologian teaching at Regent College in Vancouver, has offered an academic monograph on the *nouvelle théologie* as well as a popularly accessible book that calls for an evangelical recovery of what he calls a sacramental ontology from the patristic and medieval era.[17] Boersma goes quite a bit further than Williams, suggesting a very particular ontology as the most promising aspect of retrieval. Both have marshaled this call, however, for an "evangelical *ressourcement*" and both intend it to involve a broad retrieval of not only the theological or doctrinal, but also the exegetical and liturgical resources of the church.

The Emerging or Emergent Church(es)

Throughout the 2000s the emerging church received a massive amount of attention from church leaders, especially in North America. While much of the energy surrounding this movement involved an intentional effort to minister to people in a purportedly new postmodern era, a good deal of the literature and focus of this movement involved retrieval of various practices, texts, and ideas from the Christian past. Ranging from Celtic spirituality to patristic liturgical practices, the emerging church sought to recover certain practices from what was

15. See, most recently, D. H. Williams, *Evangelicals and Tradition: The Formative Influence of the Early Church* (Grand Rapids: Baker Academic, 2005).

16. D. H. Williams, *Retrieving the Tradition and Renewing Evangelicalism: A Primer for Suspicious Protestants* (Grand Rapids: Eerdmans, 1999).

17. Hans Boersma, Nouvelle Théologie *and Sacramental Ontology: A Return to Mystery* (New York: Oxford University Press, 2009); Hans Boersma, *Heavenly Participation: The Weaving of a Sacramental Tapestry* (Grand Rapids: Eerdmans, 2011).

viewed as the long-lost treasures of the church. Over time it became apparent that there was a sizable difference between what might be called the "emerging church" and the more radical "emergent church" (identified largely with the Emergent Village online).[18] The way in which emerging churches sought to draw on the past also proved very controversial, in that they fell prey to charges of picking and choosing as they wished and in that (at least in the more emboldened versions that go under the name "emergent") they tended toward revisionism in many ways regarding theology, ethics, and ministry practices.

Ressourcement *Thomism*

Over the last few years a number of Roman Catholic theologians have again sought to recover the Christian past for the sake of renewal. Unlike de Lubac and Congar, however, their primary emphasis has not been patristic and medieval exegesis. Theologians like Matthew Levering, Gilles Emery, and Reinhard Hütter have encouraged a renewed focus upon the theology of St. Thomas Aquinas, reading him within the deeper exegetical and theological streams of patristic theology.[19] Hütter has described the movement in this way: "These are students of the *doctor communis*, Thomas Aquinas, who seek a coherent and rigorous Catholic theological inquiry that has the intellectually and spiritually formative power of a school. They are in conversation with biblical exegesis and intentional about receiving the documents of Vatican II in a spirit of renewal and development." But they are not only students of Thomas: "This emerging Thomist *Ressourcement* is aware of a certain tendency in all schools to become narrow, and it seeks to avoid this danger by pursuing its work in dialogue with Protestant theology and with Jewish and Muslim thought."[20] *Ressourcement* Thomists have written largely in advanced academic formats, though they have addressed a wide spectrum of

18. For analysis, see Jim Belcher, *Deep Church: A Third Way Beyond Emerging and Traditional* (Downers Grove, IL: InterVarsity, 2009).

19. Reinhard Hütter and Matthew Levering, eds., *Ressourcement Thomism: Sacred Doctrine, the Sacraments, and the Moral Life* (Washington, DC: Catholic University of America Press, 2010).

20. Reinhard Hütter, "The Ruins of Discontinuity," *First Things* 209 (January 2011): 41.

issues (ranging from biblical exegesis to liturgics to ethics, as well as matters of dogmatic theology).

As can be seen here, retrieval seems to be afoot in various ways.[21] Of course these movements sometimes coalesce, sometimes diverge, and sometimes inevitably conflict with one another. We hope that seeing the panoply of ways in which the catholic tradition is being retrieved piques your interest, but we also hope that seeing the diverse ways in which this *ressourcement* occurs prompts your concern for think-ing about a principled way to do so. Unfortunately, many Protestant programs of retrieval to date cannot seem to get beyond practicing a kind of "theological bricolage." That is to say, the various rationales for appropriating this or that bit of the catholic tradition are either (ironically) not catholic enough—that is, they are independent acts of reasoning rather than acts of reasoning in and with the church—or they are not evangelical enough—that is, they are unable to muster distinctly Protestant reasons for appropriating the catholic tradition of the church. We are convinced therefore that there is need for a programmatic assessment of what it means to retrieve the catholic tradition of Christianity on the basis of Protestant theological and ecclesiological principles.

The Movement of This Manifesto

Reformed catholicity is a theological sensibility, not a system. And this book is merely a manifesto, not a full-blown theological meth-odology. This book, therefore, does not address every topic or theme involved in describing a prolegomena to theology or the foundations of Christian faith and practice. This book is a volley in an ongoing discussion about the way in which Christians and churches do theology and offer their lives as living sacrifices. It is rooted in a theological judgment about where theology in the West stands in the twenty-first century and wagers that, at this moment at least, theology stands in

---

21. Todd Billings mentions still further movements in the English-speaking world in the afterword of this volume. We might mention only one example in another linguistic context: G. Van den Brink and C. van der Kooi, *Christelijke Dogmatiek: Een Inleiding* (Zoetermeer: Boekencentrum, 2012), which offers a lengthy analysis of the churchly and catholic nature of the Christian life (501–53).

particularly acute need of resources from the Christian past if it is to find renewal. It also wagers that we need to approach this process of remembrance with theological acuity. Not every form of retrieval or every case of remembrance will be helpful.

Our thesis is that there are Reformed theological and ecclesiological warrants for pursuing a program of retrieval, that we can and should pursue catholicity on Protestant principles, and that pursuing this path holds promise for theological and spiritual renewal. We do not claim to have found in the Reformed tradition specifically or in the broader Protestant tradition more generally a fully developed dogmatics of *ressourcement*. Martin Chemnitz's *Examination of the Council of Trent* or John Jewel's *Apology of the Church of England* perhaps come the closest to providing the elements for developing such a framework.[22] However, we do believe that classical Reformed thought, both in the era of the Reformation and beyond in the era of Reformed Orthodoxy, provide numerous *examples* of thoughtful appropriation of the catholic tradition and, moreover, that the *principles* of classical Reformed orthodox prolegomena, as well as the principles of classical Reformed ecclesiology, provide a salutary framework within which a Reformed dogmatics of retrieval might be developed.[23]

Again, our purpose here is not to develop a full-blown dogmatics of retrieval but rather to offer exploratory excursions into some of the major theological places where we have found examples and principles of Reformed theology that might commend an embrace of Christian tradition (both catholic and Protestant). We will proceed as follows.

First, "Learning Theology in the School of Christ" (chap. 1) sketches a theological portrait of the way in which the catholic church is the context for doing theology. Retrieval is not merely a pragmatic maneuver or strategic approach to hermeneutical analysis or ministry philosophy. Retrieval is a mode of intellectual and spiritual operation because it fits well with the divine economy and the principles of

22. Martin Chemnitz, *Examination of the Council of Trent*, 4 vols., trans. Fred Kramer (St. Louis: Concordia, 1971); John Jewel, *Apology of the Church of England*, ed. Henry Morley (London: Cassell, 1888).

23. See, for example, Irena Backus, ed., *The Reception of the Church Fathers in the West: From the Carolingians to the Maurists*, 2 vols. (Leiden: Brill, 1996).

theology. Postmodern and contextualist approaches to epistemology and communication theory may tend toward an appreciation for reception history, but such are at best secular parables of the truth. Christians and churches need a theological argument for a catholic and Reformed theology: our methodology ought not simply shift with the rising and falling of various academic and cultural fads. This chapter, then, offers a Christology and pneumatology that positions the catholic location wherein God reforms his people.

Second, nothing so undermines the work of good theological retrieval as common misperceptions about the Protestant doctrine of *sola Scriptura*. In two chapters we seek to retrieve this doctrine, prying away some modern malformations and returning to the catholic context of its original advocates. First, we consider what *sola Scriptura* meant to its classic formulations (chap. 2). By looking at figures like Martin Bucer and texts like the early Reformed confessions, we consider the powerful claims made by this slogan as well as the limits of its import. Second, we consider biblical traditioning, that is, the biblical insistence that we not read the Bible by itself (chap. 3). Indeed the more committed one is to biblical authority for faith and practice, the more one is compelled (by the Bible's own teaching) to honor other authorities in the life of the Christian and of the church.

Third, a particular way in which the catholic shape of the church is meant to shape our lives and witness is by the exercise of churchly authority in the function of ecclesial confessions. In "A Ruled Reading Reformed" (chap. 4), we consider the hermeneutical function of the authoritative texts of the Christian church.

Fourth, no modern challenge so runs against the functioning of tradition as the divide between biblical and theological studies in the modern academy. Modern specialization has only exacerbated a divide that was breached initially for political reasons, namely, to seek peace by reading the canonical writings in an objective or historical (rather than dogmatic or confessional) way. "In Defense of Proof Texting" (chap. 5) attempts to tackle and traverse this divide and turns to one feature of classic theological work, the proof text reference, as a sign and symbol of a different vision of theological culture. The proof text, at its best, signals a symbiotic relationship between commentarial specificity and dogmatic synthesis as well as exegetical precision and confessional cognizance. We describe the way in which proof texts helped shape the theological program of Thomas Aquinas and John Calvin, arguing that there are many lessons to be gained not only from what these spiritual ancestors believed but also from how they went about doing theology.

The book concludes with an afterword by J. Todd Billings. His plea for "rediscovering the Catholic-Reformed tradition for today" sums up the sensibilities of this manifesto and connects the vision of Reformed catholicity with congregational life on the ground. Billings contrasts the notion of a catholic and Reformed tradition with the piety of common American religion (what Christian Smith has called "moralistic therapeutic deism"). Further, he compares two visions of congregational ministry, juxtaposing the ministry of a church shaped by consumerism with another intentionally devoted to Reformed catholicity in the city.

1

Learning Theology
in the School of Christ

The Principles of Theology
and the Promise of Retrieval

A program of retrieval in theology rests upon the judgment that modern theology exhibits "a stubborn tendency to grow not higher but to the side,"[1] and that the path toward theological renewal lies in moving from "a less profound to a more profound tradition; a discovery of the most profound resources."[2] Moving into such a tradition, discovering such resources, requires the cultivation of attitudes and practices that have not been especially prominent in modern

1. To borrow Alexander Solzhenitsyn's language in "The Relentless Cult of Novelty," Catholic Education Resource Center, 1993, http://www.catholiceducation.org/articles/arts/al0001.html.

2. Yves Congar, *Vraie et fausse réforme dans l'Église*, Unam Sanctum 20 (Paris: Cerf, 1950), 601–2, cited in Gabriel Flynn, "Introduction: The Twentieth-Century Renaissance in Catholic Theology," in *Ressourcement: A Movement for Renewal in Twentieth-Century Catholic Theology*, ed. Gabriel Flynn and Paul D. Murray (Oxford: Oxford University Press, 2012), 4.

Protestant theology, such as a certain receptivity toward the church's past, particularly its normative creedal and confessional deliverances, and a willingness to engage in self-consciously theological and spiritual patterns of biblical interpretation, including those that many moderns have deemed useless for obtaining theological understanding. This in turn requires reconsidering the relationship between key elements in the economy of salvation (which is also the economy of theological intelligence): preeminent here is the relationship between Scripture and tradition and the varying levels of authority that a properly construed understanding of that relationship implies.

In later chapters, we will direct our attention to some of these practices and relationships. Before doing so, it is important to consider a more fundamental topic. *Ressourcement*, properly conceived, is not driven merely by a traditionalist or communal sensibility in theology. The deepest warrants for a program of retrieval are trinitarian and christological in nature. Formally stated, they concern the relationship between the principles of theology and the church, specifically, the relationship between the Spirit of Christ (the *principium cognoscendi internum* or internal cognitive principle of theology) and the renewed mind of the church (the *principium elicitivum* or elicitive principle of theology).

That relationship, and its immediate promise for a program of retrieval, may be stated as follows: Christian theology flourishes in the school of Christ, the social-historical reality to which the apostolic promise applies: "But the anointing that you received from him abides in you, and you have no need that anyone should teach you. But as his anointing teaches you about everything, and is true, and is no lie—just as it has taught you, abide in him" (1 John 2:27). Because the anointing of Christ dwells within the church, the church is *the school of Christ*. The Spirit of Christ teaches the church in sufficient and unmixed verity such that the church need not seek theological understanding from any other source or principle. Moreover, because the anointing of Christ dwells within the church, the church is *the seedbed of theology*, the fertile creaturely field within which alone Christ's teaching has the promise of flourishing in renewed human understanding. By the Spirit's presence the church has been born of God (1 John 2:29). The church thus possesses the heavenly principle of spiritual life, knowledge, and love (1 John 3:9), which enables it to see and to enter the kingdom of heaven (John 3:3, 5). By the Spirit's presence the church is equipped to discern and receive the truth confessed by the apostles (1 John 4:6; with 1 John 1:1–3) and to test and reject the spirit of false prophecy (1 John 4:1). Because the church alone has received these gifts, we should not expect theological understanding to flourish in any other field: "the world cannot receive" the Spirit of truth "because it neither sees him nor knows him" (John 14:17).

The preceding characterizations of the church are not indications of its intrinsic wisdom or academic prestige: among the called, not many are wise, not many are powerful (1 Cor. 1:26). These characterizations, rightly understood, indicate the measure of Christ's gifts and the strength of Christ's power to cause his gifts to flourish within the church. "The Spirit and the gifts are ours through him who with us sideth."[3] Nor do the preceding characterizations of the church prescribe or preclude a specific institutional setting for theology, say, the seminary or the modern research university. Rather these characterizations serve to identify the social and intellectual culture whose questions and commitments, texts and traditions, attitudes and aspirations direct and enable the pursuit of divine wisdom under the Spirit's tutelage. The unsearchable riches of Christ are made known *here*: "with all the saints" (Eph. 3:18).

What follows is a dogmatic amplification of the preceding claims and, accordingly, evangelical warrant for a program of retrieval in theology. The discussion will unfold in three steps. First, through interaction with recent discussion of the relationship between church and theology, we will attempt to identify some desiderata for establishing specifically Protestant warrants for a program of retrieval. Second, we will consider the identity of the Spirit of truth—the "anointing" of Christ—who, with the Father and the Son, is the principle and source of theology; and we will consider the nature of his illuminating presence in and with the church. Third, we will suggest that the relationship between the Spirit and the church's renewed reason

3. Martin Luther, "A Mighty Fortress Is Our God," in *Trinity Hymnal*, rev. ed. (Suwanee, GA: Great Commission Publications, 1990), no. 92.

constitutes the church's intellectual culture as a sign and instrument of the Spirit's illuminating presence.

Tradition as Divine Institution

Modern Protestant theology has not always been amenable to a churchly approach to theology. Philip Schaff identified "rationalism" and "sectarism" as two peculiarly nineteenth-century Protestant impediments to such an approach.[4] The former impediment blocks the path to heavenly wisdom by requiring theology to accommodate its material claims and interpretive methods to that which natural reason can discern or interpret on its own.[5] The latter blocks the path to heavenly wisdom by cutting itself off from the communion of saints extended through time, whether through individualist or sectarian isolation.[6]

Of course much has changed since Schaff rendered his diagnosis of modern Protestant Christianity—as the introduction to the present book bears out. The last several decades have witnessed increasing awareness among scientists, philosophers, and theologians of various ideological commitments that knowledge and the attainment of knowledge have an intrinsically social and historical dimension and therefore that the pursuit of excellence in any field of knowledge requires apprenticeship to a tradition: its normative texts, perennial puzzles, and ultimate aims. One cannot make real progress in the quest for understanding apart from a tradition.[7]

4. Philip Schaff, *The Principle of Protestantism: As Related to the Present State of the Church*, trans. J. W. Nevin (Chambersburg, PA: German Reformed Church, 1845).

5. It is a strange irony, therefore, given his rationalist commitments, that Johann P. Gabler is regularly cited by contemporary evangelicals as a model for theological encyclopedia (how to distinguish/relate biblical theology and systematic theology) and theological method (how to construct systematic theology out of biblical theology).

6. For the pervasive effects of individualism on contemporary American evangelicalism, see Christian Smith, *The Bible Made Impossible: Why Biblicism Is Not a Truly Evangelical Reading of Scripture* (Grand Rapids: Brazos, 2011), esp. chap. 1.

7. Thomas S. Kuhn, *The Structure of Scientific Revolutions*, 3rd ed. (Chicago: University of Chicago Press, 1996); Alasdair MacIntyre, *Whose Justice? Which Rationality?* (Notre Dame: University of Notre Dame Press, 1989); and Alasdair MacIntyre, *God, Philosophy, Universities: A Selective History of the Catholic Philosophical Tradition* (Lanham, MD: Rowan & Littlefield, 2011).

There are significant Christian reasons for affirming this point.[8] The Bible mandates the social and historical transmission of apostolic truth under the reign of the risen Christ (Eph. 4:11–16; 2 Tim. 2:2); also, the promise of the Spirit, and of spiritual understanding, applies not only to individuals but also to succeeding generations of God's people (Isa. 59:21; Acts 2:39). Indeed, the social reception and transmission of theology is the creaturely correlate of the unsearchable greatness of God: because the Lord is great and greatly to be praised, he must be praised in all places and at all times; one generation shall commend his works to another and shall declare his mighty acts (Pss. 145:3–4; 113:3). The fact that tradition can err does not disqualify its status as a divine institution. The abuse of a divine institution does not rule out its proper use. In the case of this institution the principle applies as well: grace restores and perfects nature.[9]

Nearly thirty years ago, George Lindbeck underlined the significance of the present point for Protestant theology with the publication of his widely acclaimed book *The Nature of Doctrine*.[10] Therein, Lindbeck argued that the acquisition of theological understanding is never merely a matter of grasping doctrinal assertions or of experiencing religious feelings. Rather, acquisition of theological understanding involves being socialized within a specific theological culture, learning what this culture means when it asserts "Jesus is Lord" (and what it doesn't mean), and learning to enter into this culture's peculiar experience of the grace of God in Christ. Theology, according to Lindbeck, is a "cultural-linguistic" phenomenon: a rule-governed form of thought, feeling, and behavior that is irreducibly and concretely communal in nature.

What Lindbeck didn't address in his book, at least to the satisfaction of many, was the theological or metaphysical basis for his claims about the nature of theology. Is Lindbeck's proposal perhaps a form of religious pluralism—"This is how I see things *from here*,

8. For further discussion, see Stephen R. Holmes, *Listening to the Past: The Place of Tradition in Theology* (Grand Rapids: Baker Academic, 2002), chaps. 1–2.

9. This point is well emphasized by Herman Bavinck throughout his dogmatics. See, for example, *Reformed Dogmatics*, vol. 1, *Prolegomena*, ed. John Bolt, trans. John Vriend (Grand Rapids: Baker Academic, 2003), 362, 493, 605.

10. George Lindbeck, *The Nature of Doctrine: Religion and Theology in a Post-liberal Age* (Louisville: Westminster John Knox, 1984).

and that's OK"? Though some have read him this way, this does not reflect Lindbeck's intention.[11] Still, the theological question remains: How are we to articulate the social and historical nature of theology as a churchly enterprise in a manner that doesn't merely amount to a defense of custom, which may well be simply the history of error, rather than a defense of tradition, the faithful transmission of apostolic truth through time?

Enter Reinhard Hütter. Hütter's book *Suffering Divine Things* (written while he was still Protestant)[12] represents a full-scale attempt to address the shortcomings of Lindbeck's proposal by providing a sophisticated dogmatic answer to the predicament that concludes the previous paragraph. We may summarize Hütter's basic response to this predicament in his own words: "Pneumatology without ecclesiology is empty, ecclesiology without pneumatology is blind."[13] According to Hütter, whereas ecclesiology provides the concrete "public" of the Spirit's work as teacher—the visible, social manifestation of the knowledge of God in the form of the church's doctrine, worship, and mission—pneumatology provides the metaphysical guarantee that the church's doctrine, worship, and mission are indeed divine and not merely human cultural products—"tradition" and not merely "custom."

We may more fully appreciate Hütter's theological and metaphysical shoring up of Lindbeck's project by setting it within the context of two of Hütter's other dialogue partners: Erik Peterson and Karl Barth,[14] both of whom attempt to spell out an account of the church's status as the school of Christ by theologically describing the relationship between church and Trinity, albeit in two very different ways. Peterson, the Roman Catholic theologian, conceives a relationship of "strict continuation" between the Incarnate Logos and the social and intellectual

11. Bruce D. Marshall, "Absorbing the World: Christianity and the Universe of Truths," in *Theology and Dialogue: Essays in Conversation with George Lindbeck*, ed. Bruce D. Marshall (Notre Dame: University of Notre Dame Press, 1990), 69–102; Bruce D. Marshall, "'We Shall Bear the Image of the Man of Heaven': Theology and the Concept of Truth," *Modern Theology* 11 (January 1995): 93–117.

12. Reinhard Hütter, *Suffering Divine Things: Theology as Church Practice*, trans. Doug Scott (Grand Rapids: Eerdmans, 2000).

13. Ibid., 127.

14. Here we leave aside the question of whether Hütter's reading of Peterson and Barth is accurate.

practices of the church.[15] Hütter, however, finds this view problematic, because it fails to account for the ongoing sinfulness of the church.[16] Barth, the Protestant theologian, conceives the relationship between the Spirit and the church as one of "fundamental diastasis . . . in which the various elements, although certainly related to one another, nonetheless remain strictly separated within this relationship."[17] The problem with Barth's view, according to Hütter, is that by separating the Spirit's theological activity in the world (which is largely internal to the human being on Hütter's reading) from the church's concrete theological culture, Barth reduces the "mediate forms" of the church's theological understanding (e.g., its creeds, confessions, etc.) to the level of human artifact alone rather than identifying them as products of coordinated divine and creaturely action.[18]

Hütter's alternative—which seeks to avoid both Peterson's "strict continuation" and Barth's "fundamental diastasis"—is pneumatological in nature. According to Hütter, the church with its social and historical doctrinal practices is "enhypostatic" in the Spirit.[19] In other words, the Spirit is the personal subject or agent of these ecclesiastical practices. Consequently, theology is fundamentally "pathic" rather than "poetic" in nature, a *receiving* of the Spirit's gifts of wisdom and understanding in and through church practices rather than a free creation of the human spirit. On Hütter's scheme, because the Spirit is the ultimate subject of the church's theological culture, we may be confident that participation in this culture will lead us to theology's ultimate aim, the knowledge and love of the Triune God.

How might we respond to the preceding discussion?[20] We will attempt to summarize the positive contribution of Hütter's proposal

15. Hütter, *Suffering Divine Things*, 104.

16. Ibid., 102.

17. Ibid., 104.

18. Ibid., 104–5, 112–13.

19. Classical post-Chalcedonian Christology affirmed that the Son of God "personalized" the human nature he assumed in the incarnation (i.e., his human nature is "enhypostatic" in the Logos) and that his human nature was "impersonal" apart from its assumption by the Son of God in the incarnation (i.e., his human nature is "anhypostatic" apart from the Logos).

20. Here we should mention Kevin J. Vanhoozer's significant response to Lindbeck and Hütter's proposals, *The Drama of Doctrine: A Canonical-Linguistic Approach to Christian Theology* (Louisville: Westminster John Knox, 2005). Vanhoozer's

in a moment. For now, we must register two concerns. First, we question the application of the christological concept of enhypostasis to pneumatological and ecclesiological realities, as this seems to compromise the *sui generis* nature of the Son's relationship to the human nature he assumed in the incarnation. Second, and following from the previous point, we worry that this "personalization" of the church's practices in the Spirit at once blurs the distinction between the divine Spirit and the spirit of the church while actually diminishing the full creaturely density and therefore responsibility of the church's being and action.

Does this leave us with Barth's "fundamental diastasis" between Spirit and church, where the church's theological culture is relegated to the status of one intellectual culture among many, and where, for example, the creeds of the church are to be privileged in biblical exegesis no more than other contemporary interpretive schemes produced by the scholarly guild (e.g., "salvation-historical" or "apocalyptic" approaches)? Not necessarily. But to see why this is the case, we need to draw upon some tracts of Protestant teaching that Barth was reluctant to employ and that he in fact criticized in his dogmatics.

Before doing so, however, it will be helpful to take stock of Hütter's contribution to our own argument for retrieval. We believe Hütter's work suggests two desiderata for a Reformed program of retrieval.

Hütter's first contribution lies in retrieving a lost Protestant sensibility regarding the relationship between church and theology. Drawing specifically upon Luther's "On the Councils and the Church" from 1539, Hütter has unearthed a Protestant theology that ties the Spirit's work of sanctification to core practices of the church such as preaching, baptism, the Lord's Supper, church discipline, ordination and office, the various activities of public worship (including prayer, praise, thanksgiving, and instruction), and discipleship.[21] Significant for Hütter's argument is that, according to Luther, "The economic

---

argument is complementary to our own, with two small caveats: (1) while Vanhoozer grounds his proposal in the trinitarian economy of salvation, our focus is also upon the intratrinitarian basis of theology; (2) we remain unconvinced that the categories Vanhoozer develops out of the dramatic metaphor (e.g., "Masterpiece Theater," "Regional Theater," "Local Theater") provide the most instructive concepts for appreciating the function of creeds and confessions in Christian theology.

21. Hütter, *Suffering Divine Things*, 128–29.

mission of the Holy Spirit, its soteriological work of sanctification and renewal, is performed *through* these seven activities."[22] These practices are "constitutive for the mode of enactment of the Holy Spirit's economic mission and thus for the church itself."[23] By retrieving Luther's concrete pneumatological ecclesiology, Hütter helps us appreciate that Reformation-era Protestantism had not yet fallen prey to the bifurcation between the work of the Spirit and the external and ordinary ecclesiastical processes of acquiring and transmitting knowledge that would afflict later modern thought.[24]

Indeed, looking beyond Luther, we see the point confirmed in the Reformed tradition as well. This is evident, not only in its doctrine of the external and ordinary means of grace, but also more broadly in its appropriation of the products and processes of the church's catechetical tradition—specifically, the use of the Creed, the Ten Commandments, and the Lord's Prayer—to instruct Christians at all levels of learning (from the cradle to the university) in the virtues of faith, hope, and love. We see in these doctrines and practices a form of Protestantism that, rather than constituting an absolute break from the intellectual and spiritual culture of the catholic church, represents a new development within that culture and a redeployment of that culture's processes and products of learning to achieve that culture's end: the knowledge and love of the Triune God.[25]

This leads to our first desideratum: *a Reformed theology of retrieval must help us perceive the processes and products by which the church receives and transmits apostolic teaching not simply as human cultural activities and artifacts but also as fruits of the Spirit.* For understandable historical and contextual reasons related to their polemics with Rome, Reformed theology historically did not provide a fully developed theology of church tradition as the "public" context of theology. Reformed theology did, however, articulate theological principles whereby such a theology of church tradition could be developed.

22. Ibid., 129 (emphasis original).
23. Ibid., 132.
24. For theological analysis of this bifurcation, see Kathryn Tanner, *Christ the Key* (Cambridge: Cambridge University Press, 2010), chap. 7.
25. Examples of this appropriation occur throughout the major eras of Reformed theology, from Heinrich Bullinger's *Decades* to the Heidelberg Catechism to Herman Witsius's commentaries on the Apostles' Creed and the Lord's Prayer.

Drawing upon these principles, we hope to lay the groundwork for a theological account of church tradition in what follows.

Hütter's second major contribution lies in rightly identifying the doctrinal *locus* that must be addressed most directly in developing a theology of the church's intellectual culture, namely, pneumatology. Hütter's missteps in construing the Spirit-church relation, however, suggest a second desideratum: *a Reformed theology of retrieval requires a pneumatology of the Spirit as teacher that rightly conceives both his distinction from and relation to the church and its theological culture.*[26]

In the sections that follow, we will seek to address these two desiderata in reverse order. In "The Spirit of Truth" we will address the second desideratum by reflecting upon the identity of the Spirit of truth, who "teaches" the church and who "abides" with the church according to Christ's promise (1 John 2:27). And in "'In your light do we see light': The Promise of Ecclesial Theology" we will address the first desideratum by considering how the Spirit's abiding presence as teacher assures that the cultural products and processes whereby the church receives and transmits doctrine can indeed be conceived as fruits of the Spirit.

The Spirit of Truth

It is tempting to begin our discussion of the Spirit's identity as teacher *in medias res* with a discussion of his temporal mission to indwell the church as teacher rather than with his eternal identity as the Spirit of truth who proceeds from the Father and the Son.[27] To do so, however, would be to risk missing that which gives the Spirit's presence its pedagogical prestige and potency. Not every spirit that has gone out

---

26. Here we wish to develop John Webster's suggestion that Protestantism not be understood "as segregating the supernatural from the natural" or "as denying any stable or enduring presence of the former in the latter" but rather "as following through the logic of the distinction between uncreated and created . . . in thinking about the church and its existence in time" (John Webster, "*Ressourcement* Theology and Protestantism," in Gabriel Flynn and Paul D. Murray, eds., *Ressourcement: A Movement for Renewal in Twentieth-Century Catholic Theology* [Oxford: Oxford University Press, 2012], 491).

27. Cf. Hütter, *Suffering Divine Things*.

into the world is the Spirit *of* God; and it is only the Spirit of God who may be regarded as the Spirit of truth (1 John 4:1–6; see also 1 Cor. 2:9–13). So that we might avoid this risk, we will order our discussion to the order of being: first, we will consider the identity of the Spirit as teacher in terms of his eternal relation to the Father and the Son; second, we will consider (briefly) the identity of the Spirit as teacher in terms of his abiding presence within the church. Such an approach will demonstrate how the church's reception and transmission of divine teaching follows "from God's self-knowledge" and is "shaped by his self-manifestation," how "reproductive intelligence" follows "productive intelligence."[28]

The Spirit of Truth's Person and Presence

We may expect to learn the mind of Christ within the school of Christ preeminently because the one who dwells within that school as teacher is himself the untaught source (*principium*) of theology. "Who has measured the Spirit of the Lord, or what man shows him his counsel? Whom did he consult, and who made him understand? Who taught him the path of justice, and taught him knowledge, and showed him the way of understanding?" (Isa. 40:13–14). The answer, of course, is "no one." With the Father and the Son, the Spirit alone is the untutored author of divine wisdom who alone comprehends the immeasurable depths of divine wisdom (Rom. 11:33; 1 Cor. 2:10–11). Didymus the Blind ably summarizes biblical teaching on the Spirit's identity in this regard: "He will not teach as an instructor or teacher of a discipline which has been learned from another. For this method pertains to those who learn wisdom and the other arts by means of study and diligence. Rather, as he himself is the art, the teaching, the wisdom, and the Spirit of truth, he invisibly imparts knowledge of divine things to the mind."[29] The Spirit's identity as the sovereign source of theological understanding must be described under a twofold aspect if we are to appreciate its full trinitarian integrity. We may appreciate

28. John Webster, *The Domain of the Word: Scripture and Theological Reason* (London: T&T Clark, 2012), 135–36.
29. Didymus the Blind, *On the Holy Spirit*, in *Works on the Holy Spirit: Athanasius and Didymus*, trans. Mark DelCogliano, Andrew Radde-Gallwitz, and Lewis Ayres (Yonkers, NY: St. Vladimir's Seminary Press, 2011), 187.

this twofold aspect of the Spirit's eternal identity by means of a brief commentary on Jesus's promise to the apostles in John 16:13–15.[30]

John 16:13–15 indicates the intratrinitarian reality that energizes the apostolic witness (of which Holy Scripture is the literary expression). According to Jesus, the mission of the disciples draws its potency from the mission of the Spirit: because "the Spirit of truth comes" to the disciples and guides them "into all the truth" (John 16:13), the disciples will be able to fulfill their apostolic commission of bearing witness to Christ (John 15:26–27). The mission of the Spirit toward the disciples, in turn, draws its potency from the Spirit's procession from the Son: The Spirit is capable of leading the disciples into all the truth because he does not speak ἀφ' ἑαυτοῦ—"from himself"; rather "whatever he hears he will speak" (John 16:13). The Spirit receives *from* the Son, and so declares what he receives *to* the disciples (John 16:14). How are we to understand this?

It might seem overly speculative to speak of an intratrinitarian reality in relation to this text. Is not the focus of this text the "economic Trinity"? The question fails to perceive the nature of the Spirit's economic mission and therefore the significance of what this text has to say about the Spirit.[31] The Spirit's activity in the economy of salvation is not separate from his immanent identity. The former is not an external, visible instance of some alternative, internal, invisible reality that we can only identify through transcendental deduction. Rightly understood, the Spirit's activity in the economy, his mission, is the temporal extension and manifestation (to the eyes of faith) of his eternal procession. To be sure, this temporal extension and manifestation is a matter of the Spirit's free and gracious self-giving: the economy in no way establishes the Spirit's eternal identity; it rather establishes the Spirit's free and gracious relation to us. Nevertheless, the Spirit's free relation to us is nothing other than the extension and expression of his internal relation to the Father and the Son usward,

30. Our comments upon this text are deeply influenced by those of Didymus the Blind, *On the Holy Spirit*, 189–96; and Thomas Aquinas, *Commentary on the Gospel of John, Chapters 13–21*, trans. Fabian Larcher (Washington, DC: Catholic University Press of America, 2010), 142–47.

31. NB: retiring the language of the "immanent Trinity" and the "economic Trinity" might serve the avoidance of this common misunderstanding.

an embracing of temporal creatures within his eternal movement and energy. The Spirit's temporal "whither" (his economic mission) includes and expresses his eternal "whence" (his eternal procession).[32]

With this clarification in mind, we may better perceive the twofold identification of the Spirit in this text. First, this text identifies the Spirit with the selfsame divine truth that characterizes the Father and the Son: he is "the Spirit of truth" (John 16:13) who holds all truth in common with the Son and with the Father: "He will glorify me, for he will take what is mine and declare it to you. All that the Father has is mine; therefore I said that he will take what is mine and declare it to you" (John 16:14–15). Truth, according to the Johannine witness, is a notion with "metaphysical heft."[33] Katherine Sonderegger summarizes this notion with characteristic eloquence:

> Truth is not simply a property of certain propositions—that the whole, say, is greater than a part—not simply a state of affairs for which sufficient evidence can be marshaled—that Abraham Lincoln was President of the United States in 1862. Truth, to speak in this ancient way, is more substantial, more exalted and transcendent, than that reached even by the scholastic "correspondence theory of truth." This time-honored definition of truth is an epistemic category—the "adequation of concept to reality," to cite Thomas Aquinas's celebrated treatment of knowledge in the *Summa Theologica*. Truth as transcendent and substantial also supersedes truth as "fact," the events and laws that hold good in our world, and in a practical and commonsense way, are true. The substantial Form of Truth radiates far beyond human knowledge as "justified true belief," to borrow one classic philosophical definition—far beyond the evidence of our senses or the deliverances of our reason. Truth, the ancients would say, simply is: Truth in the end is Reality, Being Itself, lit up from within by its own surpassing Rationality.[34]

---

32. Here we are rendering Thomas's doctrine of divine missions as summarized in *Summa Theologiae*, 1a.43. See also Gilles Emery, *The Trinitarian Theology of St. Thomas Aquinas*, trans. Francesca Aran Murphy (Oxford: Oxford University Press, 2007), chap. 15.

33. Katherine Sonderegger, "The Humility of the Son of God," in *Christology Ancient and Modern: Explorations in Constructive Dogmatics*, ed. Oliver D. Crisp and Fred Sanders (Grand Rapids: Zondervan, 2013), 64.

34. Ibid., 64.

This divine truth, we must further observe, is not something that the Spirit possesses, as a message that is distinguishable from its messenger. Truth is what the Spirit *is*: "The Spirit is the truth" (1 John 5:6; cf. John 14:6). Commenting upon the teaching in John 16:13–15 regarding the common "possession" of truth by Father, Son, and Spirit, Didymus explains:

> Now when such things are said be careful not to slip into the error of a depraved understanding and think that the Father and the Son hold some object or possession. Rather, that which the Father has substantially, that is, eternity, immutability, incorruptibility, immutable goodness subsisting of and in itself—the same things the Son has as well. . . . From this text and in the sense already established, it follows that the Son also possesses what belongs to the Father (we mentioned above what those things are), and that the Holy Spirit also possesses what belongs to the Son. For he said: *From what is mine he will receive, for this reason he will announce to you what is to come.*[35]

Second, John 16:13–15 identifies the Spirit *with* divine truth by identifying him as the Spirit *of* divine truth: the Spirit who comes to the disciples in the economy proceeds from the Father and the Son, from him who is "the only true God" (John 17:3) and from him who is "the way, and the truth, and the life" (John 14:6). The Spirit speaks as one who *hears*; the Spirit proclaims as one who *receives* (John 16:13, 14). Again, given divine simplicity, the Spirit's hearing and receiving are identical with his being: "The Holy Spirit receives from the Son that which belongs to his own nature. . . . For the Son is nothing other than those things which are given to him by the Father, and the substance of the Holy Spirit is nothing other than that which is given to him by the Son."[36] Nevertheless, while there is no distinction between the Spirit and the divine truth that he receives, there is a distinction between the Spirit and those from whom he receives it.[37] The distinction "is not in what is had, but in the order of having."[38] Consequently, when the Spirit

35. Didymus, *On the Holy Spirit*, 195–96. See also Thomas Aquinas, *Commentary on the Gospel of John, Chaps. 13–21*, 144–46.

36. Didymus, *On the Holy Spirit*, 194.

37. Aquinas, *Commentary*, 144–46.

38. Ibid., 145.

speaks and proclaims the truth to us as one who hears and receives from the Father and the Son, he acts toward us in his distinctive personal identity: "Just as the Son does not act from himself but from the Father, so the Holy Spirit, because he is from another, that is, from the Father and the Son, *will not speak from himself, but whatever he will hear* by receiving knowledge as well as his essence from eternity, *he will speak,* not in a bodily way but by enlightening your minds from within."[39]

Though we will have to spell out the significance of the present point below, it is worth noting the relationship between the Spirit's distinctive personal identity and the church's act of traditioning. Aidan Nichols describes the general rule that governs this relationship: "The relations of the divine Persons with human persons have as their purpose to manifest the divine Persons to the human persons so that the human may participate in the divine."[40] Put in terms of the present discussion: The Spirit is the "Lord of the hearing" (Karl Barth) when it comes to the reception of the gospel within the economy of salvation, because he is the Lord who hears within the internal life of the Trinity. The church's activity of receiving and transmitting apostolic truth is therefore a fellowship with the Spirit's immanent personal act of receiving and speaking the truth, an act that the Spirit extends into the economy through his temporal mission in order to embrace us within its eternal energy and movement. In Pauline idiom, because God has sent "the Spirit of his Son" into our hearts, we cry: "Abba! Father!" (Gal. 4:6). Because the one true God has sent the Spirit of truth into our hearts, we receive and profess the truth that "Jesus is Lord" (1 Cor. 12:1–3) and that "Jesus Christ has come in the flesh" (1 John 4:2, 13–14). The church's reception and transmission of its trinitarian confession is a sign and consequence of its fellowship with the Father, through the Son, in the Spirit.

We may summarize the preceding discussion and prepare ourselves for the final point of this section by identifying the Spirit as teacher in relation to three moments of divine self-knowledge and self-manifestation: (1) With the Father and the Son, the Spirit is the ontological principle (*principium essendi*) of theology. The deep source

39. Ibid., 142 (emphasis original).
40. Aidan Nichols, *The Chalice of God: A Systematic Theology in Outline* (Collegeville, MN: Liturgical, 2012), 107 (6.4.3).

of the church's theology is the Spirit's unique and unfathomable divine self-knowledge: "The Spirit searches everything, even the depths of God. For who knows a person's thoughts except the spirit of that person, which is in him? So also no one comprehends the thoughts of God except the Spirit of God" (1 Cor. 2:10–11). The divine self-knowledge of the Spirit unfolds itself, by God's free grace, in two moments of divine self-manifestation. (2) By his work of inspiration, the Spirit produces Holy Scripture, the external cognitive principle of the church's theology (*principium cognoscendi externum*). The Spirit causes the prophets and apostles first to "understand" and then to "impart" the "secret and hidden wisdom of God" in "words not taught by human wisdom but taught by the Spirit" (1 Cor. 2:7, 12–13) with the result that, in hearing the prophetic and apostolic writings, we hear "what the Spirit says to the churches" (Rev. 3:6).[41] (3) By his work of illumination, the Spirit completes the movement of divine self-manifestation by causing the divine wisdom published in the prophetic and apostolic writings to be received and confessed by the church. In his illuminating activity, the Spirit is the internal cognitive principle of the church's theology (*principium cognoscendi internum*). The Spirit causes the church to "accept the things of the Spirit of God"—things "decreed before the ages for our glory" concerning the crucifixion of "the Lord of glory"—by enabling the church spiritually to discern those things (1 Cor. 2:7–8, 14). The Spirit's activity as the internal cognitive principle of the church's theology is the subject of what follows.

The Spirit as Teacher

How shall we characterize this activity of the Spirit as the internal cognitive principle of the church's theology? We will reserve our discussion of the creaturely coordinates of divine illumination for the next section. For now, we may summarize the nature of the Spirit's abiding presence as teacher.

The Spirit of truth abides with the church as teacher in accordance with Christ's promise (1 John 2:27). Just as he led the disciples "into all

41. For further discussion, see Timothy Ward, *Words of Life: Scripture as the Living and Active Word of God* (Downers Grove, IL: IVP Academic, 2009); and Scott R. Swain, *Trinity, Revelation, and Reading: A Theological Introduction to the Bible and Its Interpretation* (London: T&T Clark, 2011), chap. 3.

the truth" (John 16:13), enabling them to bear their apostolic witness (John 15:26–27), so he teaches the church "about everything, and is true, and is no lie" (1 John 2:27), enabling the church to receive and respond to the apostolic witness (1 John 1:1–3). Although the Spirit's presence in the church as teacher completes the movement of divine self-manifestation that is rooted in God's self-knowledge, it does not complete the Spirit's being. The Spirit's being is complete within the perfect inner movement of God's triune life. The Spirit comes to the church not in order to fulfill his being but in order to fill the church with a spirit of wisdom and revelation in the knowledge of God (Eph. 1:17; 3:14–19). Nevertheless, when the Spirit comes, he comes to stay: "I will ask the Father, and he will give you another Helper, to be with you forever" (John 14:16). The Spirit's abiding presence as teacher is thus a matter of his sovereign self-determination and commitment, what we might call his "covenant identity" (Ezek. 36:27–28).[42] Because the Spirit has come to dwell with the church forever, because he has established the church upon the prophetic and apostolic witness through inspiration, and because he continues to enable the church to receive and respond to that witness through illumination, the school of Christ holds the promise of theological flourishing.

This, then, is the identity of the Spirit as teacher. And it is *his* identity as the Spirit of truth and *his* faithfulness to dwell with us forever that is the fundamental reality in the school of Christ, the infinite fountain of divine wisdom that causes the knowledge of God to flourish in our midst. Everything else that we can and must say about the promise of ecclesial theology flows from this fundamental reality.

"In your light do we see light": The Promise of Ecclesial Theology

The Spirit alone is the principle of theology, the infinite ocean and transcendent fountain of divine truth. The church is not that ocean; the church is not that fountain. Do such assertions threaten to naturalize

42. For further discussion of the theological metaphysics involved in this assertion, see Scott R. Swain, *The God of the Gospel: Robert Jenson's Trinitarian Theology*, Strategic Initiatives in Evangelical Theology (Downers Grove, IL: IVP Academic, 2013), chaps. 6–8.

the church and its theological tradition or to impose a false extrinsicism upon the God-world relation? Not necessarily. To the Spirit's identity as divine teacher there corresponds a creaturely community that is taught: "In your light do we see light" (Ps. 36:9). The Spirit, who hears and speaks the truth within God's triune life, creates, sustains, and directs a fellowship that hears and speaks the truth within history. Indeed, so effectual is the Spirit's role as teacher that the community's corresponding vocation is simply to "abide" in what it has been taught "from the beginning" (1 John 2:24; 2 John 1:5–6): it need not search about anxiously for truth or for teachers; it only needs to assume a stance of historical continuity and faithfulness in relation to the apostolic deposit that it has received by the Spirit's illuminating presence (1 John 1:1–3; 2:7). Tradition is the church's stance of abiding in and with apostolic teaching through time, the "creaturely social co-efficient"[43] of the Spirit's activity as the internal cognitive principle of theology. How shall we characterize this relationship between the Spirit who abides in the church and the church that abides in the teaching vouchsafed to it by the Spirit in Holy Scripture?

Our answer to this question will emerge in three steps. First, we will consider the relationship between Scripture and tradition that follows from Reformed theological principles. (Our discussion here will be brief since we develop this point more fully in later chapters.) Second, we will consider the nature of the creaturely coordinates that emerge within the sphere of the Spirit's pedagogical economy. Two creaturely coordinates in particular will command our attention here: the nature of created reason and of the spiritual habit by which the Spirit renews and perfects created reason. Third, following from the previous point, we will conclude with how the products and processes of the church's intellectual culture may be understood both as signs and instruments of the Spirit's illuminating work.

Scripture and Tradition

Under the influence of John Henry Newman, many Roman Catholic theologians (including Joseph Ratzinger, later Pope Benedict XVI)

---

43. John Webster, "'In the Society of God': Some Principles of Ecclesiology," in *God Without Measure* (London: T&T Clark, forthcoming).

have described the Spirit-guided relationship between Scripture and tradition by means of an organic metaphor. Tradition, on this understanding, is "the living process whereby the Holy Spirit introduces us to the fullness of truth and teaches us how to understand what previously we could still not grasp . . . yet was already handed down in the original Word."[44] According to this metaphor, the Spirit enables tradition to take what dwells "preconceptually, obscurely, and in an unformulated state" within the apostolic deposit and make it "at last explicit to illumine minds and rejoice hearts."[45] Though this construal is to be preferred to the "two-source theory" of Scripture and tradition espoused by the Council of Trent, and though Vatican II arguably gestures toward a doctrine of the material sufficiency of Scripture in relation to tradition,[46] this construal still seems to compromise the finality and sufficiency of Holy Scripture in relation to tradition.[47] On the contrary, we must confess: "Holy Scripture is *sufficient* for the instruction of the saints as they are conveyed by God towards eternal fellowship with himself. The prophets and apostles are not one element in a larger canvas, or even the most important element. Rather, in their words we have the fullness of what for now the Spirit says to the churches. Scripture is *enough.*"[48]

Some will worry that such a confession necessarily retards a fully developed theology of tradition. And, admittedly, Reformation and post-Reformation polemic against Roman Catholic doctrine can be taken as a harbinger of the Enlightenment desire to release reason from its state of self-imposed tutelage to tradition.[49] However, a rightly ordered understanding of the principles of theology will preserve us from this tendency toward a retarded conception of tradition.

44. Joseph Ratzinger, *Milestones: Memoirs 1927–1977*, trans. Erasmo Leiva-Merikakis (San Francisco: Ignatius, 1998), 58–59.
45. Nichols, *Chalice of God*, 55 (emphasis original).
46. See Thomas G. Guarino, "Catholic Reflections on Discerning the Truth of Sacred Scripture," in *Your Word Is Truth: A Project of Evangelicals and Catholics Together*, ed. Charles Colson and Richard John Neuhaus (Grand Rapids: Eerdmans, 2002), 79–101.
47. We will develop an alternative construal more fully in chaps. 2 and 3 below.
48. Webster, *Domain of the Word*, 18.
49. John Barton, "Historical-Critical Approaches," in *The Cambridge Companion to Biblical Interpretation*, ed. John Barton (Cambridge: Cambridge University Press, 1998), chap. 1.

While Holy Scripture, as *principium cognoscendi externum*, is the divinely authoritative and sufficient *source* of theology, tradition, the Spirit-enabled reception of Scripture, is the divinely appointed *goal* of theology: "the word changed into grace in our hearts."[50] None have made the point with greater clarity or consistency than Herman Bavinck:

> After Jesus completed his work, he sent forth the Holy Spirit who, while adding nothing new to the revelation, still guides the church into the truth (John 16:12–15) until it passes through all its diversity and arrives at the unity of faith and the knowledge of the Son of God (Eph. 3:18, 19; 4:13). In this sense, there is a good, true, and glorious tradition. It is the method by which the Holy Spirit causes the truth of Scripture to pass into the consciousness and life of the church. Scripture, after all, is only a means, not the goal. The goal is that, instructed by Scripture, the church will freely and independently make known "the wonderful deeds of him who called it out of darkness into his marvelous light" (1 Pet. 2:9). The external word is the instrument, the internal word the aim. Scripture will have reached its destination when all have been taught by the Lord and are filled with the Holy Spirit.[51]

Creaturely Coordinates: Renewed Reason and the Habit of Grace

Given such a positive conception of the Scripture-tradition relation, how should we conceive the creaturely coordinates of the Spirit's presence as teacher? Stated simply, tradition is the temporally extended, socially mediated activity of renewed reason: theology's *principium elicitivum*, or elicitive principle. Through the reception and transmission of what it has received from the Holy Spirit in the prophetic-apostolic embassy of Holy Scripture, renewed reason abides and flourishes within the school of Christ. We may appreciate how this is the case by considering the nature of reason and the nature of reason's renewal through the gift of a spiritual habit.

Created reason emerges within the economy of divine teaching as "a grace and gift of love."[52] As in the case of all other creatures, "Reason is

---

50. John Owen, *A Discourse Concerning the Holy Spirit*, ed. William H. Goold, vol. 3 in *The Works of John Owen* (London: Banner of Truth, 1966), 470.

51. Bavinck, *Reformed Dogmatics*, 1:493–94; see also 380, 506.

52. Webster, *Domain of the Word*, 126. For what follows, see ibid., 122–28.

created, fallen, and redeemed."[53] First, reason is *created*: "The creator endows creatures with reason in order that, hearing his intelligible word of promise and command, they may know him, and so love and obey him."[54] Reason is a grace, given to creatures made in God's image in order that they might actively and intelligently engage in covenant fellowship with their Triune Creator. Second, however, reason is also *fallen*: Reason's "nature is defiled. In the regime of sin, the structure of human desire collapses, because creatures do not give active consent to their creaturely vocation. And in the general collapse, reason also falls into futility and darkness; alienated from the life of God, it is overwhelmed by the callousness and squalor into which we betray ourselves." Alienated from the divine teacher, reason is fruitless in the knowledge of God and therefore an active agent of idolatry and immorality (see Rom. 1:18–32). Third, by God's mercy reason is *rescued and renewed*: "Like all other aspects of created being, weakened and rendered dark and futile by sin, reason is encountered by the assurance and creative power of the forgiveness of sins. Divine judgment renews; it slays in order to make alive. There is not only declension; there is a renewal in the spirit of the mind, a new creaturely nature created after the likeness of God. The gracious, sovereign movement of Word and Spirit outbids the fall."[55] In its rescue and renewal by God, reason is raised and restored to its proper function within the economy of divine teaching. In terms of the present discussion, this means that everything that the Spirit does *in* us to illumine Holy Scripture, he does *by* us, by the instrumentality of created reason in its social and historical expression.[56]

Under the sovereign sway of the Spirit's illuminating aid, created reason functions as the elicitive principle of theology (*principium elicitivum*). As elicitive principle, reason is both "the receiving subject of faith" and "the instrument and principle . . . that elicits faith and factual knowledge."[57] Thus understood, reason's vocation to abide in apostolic

---

53. Ibid., 124.
54. Ibid.
55. Ibid., 125.
56. Owen, *Discourse*, 204.
57. Gisbertus Voetius, "The Use of Reason in Matters of Faith," in Willem van Asselt et al., *Introduction to Reformed Scholasticism* (Grand Rapids: Reformed Heritage Books, 2011), 228; with Henk Van Den Belt, *The Authority of Scripture in Reformed Theology: Truth and Trust* (Leiden: Brill, 2008), 167–69.

teaching is anything but a passive enterprise. Though this vocation is rooted in the obedient reception of divine truth, it is aimed at acquisition of further knowledge through disciplined and virtuous study of Holy Scripture under the Spirit's tutelage within the communion of saints. Reason pursues its studious vocation by functioning as a "principle that draws conclusions (*principium quod*) from the only, infallible principle of the Scriptures, and so by means of simple apprehension, of composition, of division, and of discursive reasoning it achieves understanding of what is revealed supernaturally or spiritually."[58] Furthermore, though reason can only proceed in its vocation on the basis of shared communal assumptions about the nature, norms, and goals of theology, because reason is finite, and because it has not yet received its patrimony in the beatific vision, reason's vocation is "inseparable from ongoing enquiry, from reformulating old questions, testing established beliefs, asking new questions, and so providing new resources for teaching."[59] Reason's vocation is inseparable from a lively tradition of debate about what does and does not count as the faithful extension of tradition toward its goal, the knowledge and love of the Triune God.[60] Within the context of such a tradition, reason can only fulfill its vocation with the aid of the intellectual and moral virtues, spiritual requisites to reason's communal pursuit of divine wisdom in its pilgrimage from idolatry to the vision of God.[61] It is only as reason exercises and excels in these virtues by the grace of Jesus Christ, through the mortifying and vivifying power of the Spirit of Christ, that it becomes docile before its teachers and also discerning enough to distinguish doctrinal treachery from want of instruction, irreligion from immaturity, and thus is equipped to preserve the unity of the Spirit in the bond of peace as it pursues its communal calling to know and love the Triune God.

This leads us to a second creaturely coordinate of the Spirit's illuminating presence: the spiritual habit of grace that is given, sustained,

58. Voetius, "The Use of Reason in Matters of Faith," 228.

59. MacIntyre, *God, Philosophy, Universities*, 68.

60. For an instructive recent survey of diversity within the Reformed tradition and of how the Reformed tradition has managed diversity in diverse ways, see Michael A. G. Haykin and Mark Jones, eds., *Drawn into Controversie: Reformed Theological Diversity and Debates Within Seventeenth-Century British Puritanism* (Göttingen: Vandenhoeck & Ruprecht, 2011).

61. On which, see Webster, *Domain of the Word*, chaps. 8 and 10.

and directed by the Spirit in order to aid reason's sanctified exercise in the knowledge of God. In summarizing the main lines of this topic, we follow John Owen's exquisite discussion in two works, *Of Communion with God the Father, Son, and Holy Ghost* and *A Discourse Concerning the Holy Spirit*.[62]

According to Owen, in regenerating fallen human beings, the Holy Spirit plants a new spiritual habit within them, replacing the old sinful habit inherited from Adam and purged by the blood of Christ. This new spiritual habit exists preeminently and in fullest measure in Jesus Christ, the head of the new humanity, and flows to the church from Jesus Christ, who is the fountain of ectypal theology—that is, human knowledge of God.[63] Owen defines this habit as "a new, gracious, spiritual life, or principle, created, and bestowed on the soul, whereby it is changed in all its faculties and affections, fitted and enabled to go forth in the way of obedience unto every divine object that is proposed unto it."[64] This habit is distinct from the rational faculties of the soul, but it is essential to their functioning in the knowledge of God. Far from replacing our rational faculties, this new spiritual habit energizes their various operations toward God and creatures.[65] It enables the mind to discern spiritual things: "All sanctified believers have an ability and power, in the renewed mind and understanding, to see, know, discern, and receive, spiritual things, the mysteries of the gospel, the mind of Christ, in a due and spiritual manner."[66] It also enables the soul to embrace Christ by faith as he is offered in the gospel and to rest with "delight, desire, and complacency" in Christ, "being, indeed, the principle suiting all the faculties of our souls for spiritual and living operations, according to their natural use."[67] Although natural habits

62. Our analysis here is indebted to Christopher Cleveland, *Thomism in John Owen* (Farnham, UK: Ashgate, 2013), chaps. 3–4.

63. Owen, *Discourse*, 159–88, 514–19. More fully, see Willem van Asselt, "The Fundamental Meaning of Theology: Archetypal and Ectypal Theology in Seventeenth-Century Reformed Thought," *Westminster Theological Journal* 64 (2002): 319–35.

64. John Owen, *Of Communion with God the Father, Son, and Holy Ghost*, ed. William H. Goold, vol. 2 in The Works of John Owen (Edinburgh: Banner of Truth, 1965), 200.

65. Owen, *Discourse*, 168–69, 502–3.

66. Ibid., 493.

67. Ibid., 200.

may be acquired through repeated activity, this spiritual habit is a free and unsolicited gift of God: "This nature is from God, its parent; it is that in us which is born of God. And it is common unto or the same in all believers, as to its kind and being, though not as to degrees and exercise. It is that which we cannot learn, which cannot be taught us but by God only, as he teaches other creatures in whom he planteth a natural instinct."[68] And yet, while this habit is not acquired through repeated activity, because grace restores and perfects nature, this habit may be "preserved, increased, strengthened, and improved" through spiritual acts of duty and obedience.[69]

Barth expressed great reservations about appropriating the notion of habit in Protestant theology, regarding its use in older Protestant dogmatics as a "fatal" and "sinister" side-glance away from the gospel of Jesus Christ. His chief objection was that the notion of habit turned grace into a *given*, a static possession rather than an ever-new event of divine giving and human receiving.[70] We believe Barth's objection is misguided for two reasons. First (due to Barth's actualism?), it fails to appreciate that the permanence of this particular divine gift constitutes its particular modality: "God's seed *abides* in him" (1 John 3:9). Second, it also fails to appreciate that, rather than undermining the continuous, eventful nature of divine giving and human receiving, this notion in Owen's evangelical hand requires it:

> This *habit* or principle, thus wrought and abiding in us, doth not, if I may say so, firm its own station, or abide and continue in us by its own natural efficacy, in adhering unto the faculties of our souls. Habits that are acquired by many actions have a natural efficacy to preserve themselves, until some opposition that is too hard for them prevail against them; which is frequently (though not easily) done. But this is preserved in us by the constant powerful actings and influence of the Holy Ghost. He which works it in us doth also preserve it in us. And the reason hereof is, because the spring of it is in our head, Christ Jesus, it being only an emanation of virtue and power from him unto

68. Ibid., 469.
69. Ibid., 476.
70. Karl Barth, *Church Dogmatics*, vol. 4, *The Doctrine of Reconciliation*, part 2, ed. G. W. Bromiley and T. F. Torrance, trans. G. W. Bromiley (Edinburgh: T&T Clark, 1958), 89–90.

us by the Holy Ghost. If this be not actually and always continued, whatever is in us would die and wither of itself. *See* Eph. 4:15, 16; Col. 3:3; John 4:14. It is in us as the fructifying sap is in a branch of the vine or olive. It is there really and formally, and is the next cause of the fruit bearing of the branch: but it doth not live and abide by itself, but by a continual emanation and communication from the root; let that be intercepted, and it quickly withers. So is it with this principle in us, with respect unto its root, Christ Jesus.[71]

The Headship of Christ and the Church's Spiritual and Intellectual Culture

We are now in a position to draw the preceding argument to a conclusion and to suggest what it means, on Reformed theological principles, to regard the products and processes of the church's spiritual and intellectual culture as fruits of the Spirit. Doing so requires that we reflect a bit more fully on the relationship between Jesus Christ and the church.

Church tradition exists as the school of Christ, and Christian theology flourishes within the school of Christ because Jesus, the messianic Son of the living God (Matt. 16:16), has sworn a promise: "I will build my church" (Matt. 16:18). Christ lays the foundation for his church through the prophetic and apostolic witness and by the Spirit's work of inspiration: "You are Peter, and on this rock I will build my church" (Matt. 16:18; with Eph. 2:20). As we have seen, the laying of this foundation, in turn, has a goal. Christ lays the foundation of the church in the prophets and apostles in order to build upon that foundation by the Spirit's illuminating work in and through the renewed reason of the people of God: in accordance with the riches of his glory and by the strengthening power of his Spirit in the church's inner being (the *principium cognoscendi internum*), God the Father causes Jesus the messianic Son to dwell within the hearts of his people through faith, strengthening us to comprehend with all the saints the immeasurable depths of Christ's saving love (the *principium elicitivum*), filling us with all the fullness of God (Eph. 3:14–19).

71. Owen, *Discourse*, 475–76.

The relationship between Christ's foundational work through the Spirit by his prophets and apostles and Christ's constructive work through the Spirit by the church's renewed intelligence may be described under two aspects. According to Owen, Jesus Christ is the head of his body the church "in the double sense of that word": in terms of *authority*, Jesus Christ "is the political head of it in a way of rule and government"; in terms of *anointing*, Jesus Christ "is the really spiritual head, as unto vital influences of grace, unto all his members."[72] We will consider these two senses of Christ's headship in order.

First, Jesus's work of building his church is an expression of his messianic *authority*. Accordingly, the relationship between Christ and his church reflects a distinctive *pattern of authority*. Jesus, the messianic Son of Man who possesses *all* authority (Matt. 28:18), establishes in the witness of his prophets and apostles what we may call a *foundational* authority. The apostles have laid a foundation, and no one else can lay a foundation (1 Cor. 3:10–11): as Childs puts it, "We are neither prophets nor apostles."[73] This foundation, of which Holy Scripture is the literary product and deposit, is sufficient to equip the church with all it needs in order to know, love, and serve God (2 Tim. 3:16–17). All that is said or done in the church in the name of Jesus Christ is accountable to this foundation and will be measured by its faithfulness to this foundation: "Now if anyone builds on this foundation with gold, silver, precious stones, wood, hay, straw—each one's work will become manifest, for the Day will disclose it. . . . If the work that anyone has built on the foundation survives, he will receive a reward. If anyone's work is burned up, he will suffer loss, though he himself will be saved, but only as through fire" (1 Cor. 3:12–15). This is the negative correlate of *sola Scriptura*: Holy Scripture provides the supreme and sufficient foundation to which theological tradition is accountable and by which theological tradition is measured. It is the norm that norms all other norms and that is not itself normed.

There is, however, a positive correlate of *sola Scriptura* as well, a correlate that has not always received due recognition in Protestant

---

72. Ibid., 518–19.
73. Brevard S. Childs, *Biblical Theology of the Old and New Testaments: Theological Reflection on the Christian Bible* (Minneapolis: Fortress, 1993), 381.

theology. Through Holy Scripture, the church's foundational authority, the Lord who possesses all authority *authorizes the church to build* on that foundation. Again, as we have seen, the reason for laying a foundation is in order to build: Scripture is a means to the end of church tradition (Herman Bavinck). Christ not only gives prophets and apostles, he also gives evangelists, pastors, and teachers (Eph. 4:11). And he gives them in order that they might build up the body of Christ "until we all attain to the unity of the faith and of the knowledge of the Son of God, to mature manhood, to the measure of the stature of the fullness of Christ" (Eph. 4:12–13).[74] The process of receiving and transmitting apostolic truth has a *terminus a quo*, Holy Scripture, from which it flows and to which it is accountable. And the process of receiving and transmitting apostolic truth has a *terminus ad quem* to which it flows, the maturity of the saints and their obtaining the measure of the stature of the fullness of Christ. The church is authorized to pursue this end; and theology flourishes within the sphere of the church's authorized pursuit of this end.

Although the apostolic deposit cannot grow, the church's understanding of that deposit can, and indeed must, grow. The church is always poised between the alternatives of immaturity, characterized by instability and ignorance (Eph. 4:14), and maturity, characterized by stability in and knowledge of the truth (Eph. 4:13). Christ has appointed authorized instruments within the church by which the church may avoid the former and attain the latter. By the strength which the Lord its head supplies, the church *"builds itself up* in love" through the operation of these instruments (Eph. 4:15–16, emphasis added).

To cite one example: dogma is a vital instrument by which the church builds itself up in love. Donald Wood describes well the pattern of authority operative in the church's production of creeds: "Because all genuine authority is self-communicating, Scripture engenders in the reading church dogmatic statements that themselves enjoy a derivative, limited, but just so proper authority of their own."[75] As Wood observes, under Jesus's messianic rule in Holy Scripture, such

74. See Michael Horton, "Ephesians 4:1–16," in *Theological Commentary: Evangelical Perspectives*, ed. R. Michael Allen (London: T&T Clark, 2011), 129–53.
75. Donald Wood, "Some Comments on Moral Realism and Scriptural Authority," *European Journal of Theology* 18 (2009): 152.

dogmatic statements serve not only to *limit* theological and interpretive reflection but also to *enable* it: "The intention and effect of
appeals to the authority of the creeds and confessions is not simply
to close down the church's interpretive options but also to liberate
the church from merely parochial readings of Scripture—including
those readings which . . . no longer even aspire to catholicity. In this
sense, active deference to creedal and confessional documents as
authorities—secondary, derivative authorities, subject to Scripture's
absolute judgment, but authorities nonetheless—opens up theological
discourse rather than closing it down."[76] We will develop this theme
more fully in the chapters that follow, articulating the pattern of
authority that flows from Christ through Scripture to the church and
considering some of the practices of biblical reasoning that flourish
within Christ's authoritative, church-building dominion.

Second, Jesus's work of building the church is an expression of his
messianic *anointing*. Just as Christ's supreme authority establishes
a pattern of authority in the church, so Christ's supreme anointing
issues forth in an anointed community: "God who *establishes* us with
you in Christ . . . has *anointed* us" (2 Cor. 1:21, emphasis added). The
Christ who establishes and builds his church on its apostolic foundation, fills his church with every spiritual blessing by means of the
Spirit's abiding presence (Eph. 1:3, 23; 5:18). As we have seen, these
blessings include the Spirit's abiding presence as teacher and also the
effects of the Spirit's presence in the awakened activities of renewed
reason. It is time to address more directly the manner in which the
reality of this anointing informs our understanding of the products
and processes of the church's theological tradition.

Recall Hütter's concern that Barth's proposal unnecessarily sepa-
rates the Spirit's teaching activity from the church's concrete theological
culture. How does our proposal fare in relation to this concern? While
we have been determined to distinguish properly the Spirit's identity
and presence as teacher in the church from the church's reception and
transmission of apostolic teaching, we have also attempted to account
for their positive relationship and affinity. Indeed, we believe that a
failure to account for the positive relationship between the Spirit, who

76. Ibid.

is the *principium* of theology, and church tradition, which is among the Spirit's *principiata*, is a failure to honor divine wisdom and power. As the efficient and exemplary causes of theology, divine wisdom and power exhibit their perfection precisely in the production of active creaturely counterparts in the wisdom and power of the church.[77]

In light of this, we believe that the activities and artifacts of ecclesial tradition—that is, both the processes of traditioning, such as preaching and teaching, receiving the sacraments and engaging in schooling, as well as the products of traditioning, such as biblical commentaries, theological tracts, disputations, *loci communes*, creeds, and confessions—should be regarded as *natural signs* and *instruments* of the Spirit's illuminating presence. The products and processes of tradition may be regarded, first, as natural signs of the Spirit's illuminating presence not because they emerge within the order of nature; they are in fact creatures born and sustained within the order of grace. The products and processes of tradition may be regarded as natural signs of the Spirit's illuminating presence because they constitute true and proper effects of his pedagogical grace. They are fruits of the Spirit. The life-giving water that flows forth from the throne of God and of the lamb, and from the temple that Jesus Christ has founded and constructed, grows ever deeper as it proceeds, and the many trees that spring forth on its banks, along with the manifold creatures that swarm in its waters, are signs of its life-giving presence (Ezek. 47:1–10). Because "the river of the water of life" (Rev. 22:1) flows *here*, the activities and artifacts of tradition spring forth as *natural* fruits of the Spirit's life-giving presence.

The products and processes of tradition may be regarded, second, as instruments of the Spirit's illuminating presence for reasons we have already discussed. The Christ who authorizes ecclesial agents to build up the church employs these ecclesial agents as instruments in his sovereign hand (Eph. 4:15–16) and empowers these ecclesial agents in order that, through them, he might cause the church to reach the measure of the stature of the fullness of Christ. The various products and processes of church tradition are certainly fallible, and

77. See John Webster, "'Love Is Also a Lover of Life': *Creatio ex Nihilo* and Creaturely Goodness," *Modern Theology* 29 (2013): 169–70.

their existence and exercise are certainly accountable to their prophetic and apostolic foundation. Their weak and subordinate nature
notwithstanding, these instruments do not stand as obstacles to a
knowledge of God that can be gained more immediately through the
reading of Scripture without them. They stand as divinely authorized
instruments and divinely appointed aids to reading Scripture, part of
the fullness of Christ's gift that he has bestowed in and through his
anointing upon the church. Having received this anointing, and the
fruits of this anointing, the church and the church's theology can do
no better than to abide in the one who has given by abiding in the
gifts he has given (1 John 2:27).

Conclusion

In 1553, Peter Martyr Vermigli returned to the Strasbourg Academy,
having spent his past six years in Oxford as professor of theology. In
an oration on the study of theology delivered to future bishops of the
Reformed churches, he reminded his audience of the location of the
true school of theology: "The location or school of this philosophy
is in heaven; they therefore who creep along the ground and have not
made their commonwealth in heaven, as the Apostle commanded, are
in danger lest they waste their efforts in studying." He also reminded
them of the true teacher of theology: "The teacher of this subject is the
Holy Spirit. Although you will have had countless teachers, preachers,
instructors, and pedagogues, unless the Holy Spirit refashions your
inmost hearts, they will all be sweating in vain."[78]

These are the warrants for a program of retrieval in theology:
the church is the school of Christ, taught by the Spirit of Christ; the
church is the seedbed of theology that flourishes by the anointing of
Christ. We conclude our discussion with Peter Martyr's prayer that
theology may flourish in this field:

> O thrice blessed God, may the things that I am going to teach your
> disciples not be the winds of error but the needed and fruitful rains

78. Peter Martyr Vermigli, "Strasbourg Oration," in *The Peter Martyr Reader*,
ed. John Patrick Donnelly, Frank A. James III, and Joseph C. McLelland (Kirksville,
MO: Truman State University Press, 1999), 64.

of the truth. May my interpretations not be a violent rain destroying the Church and casting down consciences but a dew of consolation and a useful edification for souls. I would wish, after you have heard and answered my prayers, that all those who are here present may not listen to the sacred seed of your Word like a footpath of thorns or a rocky field. But may they be the good soil and the field prepared by your Spirit that will bring forth from the Scriptures, which have been implanted in the furrows of their hearts, fruit thirty- and sixty- and a hundredfold.[79]

79. Ibid., 66.

2

Retrieving *Sola Scriptura*, Part One

The Catholic Context of *Sola Scriptura*

Reformed catholicity might seem a project or proposal incapable of affirming the cardinal Protestant confession *sola Scriptura*. So often this slogan has represented, in the minds of its purported allies as well as its critics, a diatribe against tradition and a rebuke to the very idea of catholicity. Yet *sola Scriptura* was not intended by its original advocates in the time of the Reformation as an absolute rebuke to tradition or a denial of genuine ecclesial authority. It was a spiritual characterization of the nature of that authority and the role of that tradition. Its bastardization into a "no creed but the Bible" approach to faith and practice has followed from its being removed from its theological family: other teachings regarding God's self-communication; our receptive dependence before him in all areas of life, including the intellectual, relational, and moral; and the churchly context of such self-revelation, relational growth, and spiritual formation. *Sola Scriptura* is taken by many to involve not only a claim for the Bible but also a claim against tradition and church.

The doctrine of *sola Scriptura* must be one of the most frequently misinterpreted tracts of Christian teaching. It suffers not only from polemical mischaracterization by its critics but even from painful description from its supposed adherents. *Sola Scriptura* suffers from segmentation. Oftentimes it is pulled loose, extracted from its wider doctrinal context. In such a scenario, its true spiritual habitat is lost, and this piece of teaching is forced to address questions it cannot possibly manage to satisfy.

> An effective account of biblical authority, by contrast, will place it within a cluster of other affirmations: God as sanctifying, inspiring and authorizing presence; the Spirit as the one who enables recognition of, trust in and glad submission to the claim of Scripture's gospel content; the church as faithful, self-renouncing and confessing assembly around the lively Word of God.[1]

Here John Webster places *sola Scriptura* within a nest of doctrinal claims: first God, then the works of God in Christians and church communities. He comes around to address biblical authority, but he does so only as he identifies it as the "lively Word of God" and places it within the "faithful, self-renouncing and confessing assembly" of the church. In this chapter, following similar impulses, we want to consider the place of *sola Scriptura* within the project of Reformed catholicity. In so doing we want to listen to its critics and their concerns. We then turn to historical description of *sola Scriptura* in its Reformational articulation by individual theologians like Martin Bucer, as well as the attested exegesis of confessional statements from the sixteenth century, wherein we see that *sola Scriptura* is meant to shape engagement of the catholic tradition as a theological authority, not to foreclose such retrieval. In our investigation we confirm the claim of Todd Billings, namely, that "before *sola Scriptura* became an excuse to marginalize pre-Reformation exegesis and theology, there was another way of being Reformed."[2] More broadly, we believe that

1. John Webster, "Scripture, Church, and Canon," in *Holy Scripture: A Dogmatic Sketch*, Current Issues in Theology (Cambridge: Cambridge University Press, 2003), 55–56.
2. J. Todd Billings, "The Catholic Calvin," *Pro Ecclesia* 20, no. 2 (2011): 134. Others are offering accounts of biblical authority that affirm both the importance

commitment to *sola Scriptura* enhances our reception of the catholic fullness of the church's past.

The Danger of "Scripture Alone"

Many critics have pointed to the Reformational teaching on *sola Scriptura* as an epoch-making shift whereby ecclesiastical authority was replaced by historicism or even by subjectivism. Reformation-era historian Brad Gregory has argued that Luther and the other reformers ushered in what can only be called "the unintended reformation." He genuinely means that this secularization was unintended: "The Reformation's influence on the eventual secularization of society was complex, largely indirect, far from immediate, and profoundly unintended."[3] Gregory addresses a host of secularizing shifts, beginning with the influence of scientism and its move to marginalize God-talk from ongoing reality.

Gregory turns quickly to issues of doctrine and authority. "In Western society at large, the early twenty-first-century basis for most secular answers to the Life Questions seems to be some combination of personal preferences, inclinations, and desires: in principle truth is whatever is true to you, values are whatever you value, priorities are whatever you prioritize, and what you should live for is whatever you decide you should live for. In short: whatever."[4] Why? Why has this self-stylization taken hold of Western society? Gregory argues that the doctrine of *sola Scriptura* marginalized the role of the

---

of *sola Scriptura* as well as its catholic moorings: see especially Kevin J. Vanhoozer, *The Drama of Doctrine: A Canonical-Linguistic Approach to Christian Theology* (Louisville: Westminster John Knox, 2005); John Webster, *Holy Scripture: A Dogmatic Sketch*, Current Issues in Theology (Cambridge: Cambridge University Press, 2003); John Webster, *The Domain of the Word: Scripture and Theological Reason* (London: T&T Clark, 2012); Scott R. Swain, *Trinity, Revelation, and Reading: A Theological Introduction to the Bible and Its Interpretation* (London: T&T Clark, 2011); J. Todd Billings, *The Word of God for the People of God: An Entryway to the Theological Interpretation of Scripture* (Grand Rapids: Eerdmans, 2010); Daniel J. Treier, *Introducing Theological Interpretation of Scripture: Recovering a Christian Practice* (Grand Rapids: Baker Academic, 2008).

3. Brad S. Gregory, *The Unintended Reformation: How a Religious Revolution Secularized Society* (Harvard: Belknap, 2012), 2.

4. Ibid., 77.

church's teaching authority. It did not remove it or negate it, but it marginalized it by suggesting that it was not needful. In his historical assessment, Gregory argues that there is no meaningful distinction to be drawn between the magisterial and the radical reformers. "In no sense therefore was 'tradition' for magisterial Protestant reformers an authority to which they deferred relative to their respective readings of Scripture, as it was for their Catholic counterparts. This was the whole point and part of the power of 'scripture alone.'"[5]

Gregory continues, "Neither magisterial nor radical Protestant reformers modified their hermeneutical judgments when these were at odds with traditional authorities; instead, they rejected the latter at each point of disagreement. In principle and as a corollary of *sola Scriptura*, tradition thus retained for them *no independent* authority."[6] The Bible as illumined by the Holy Spirit was their functional authority. Where they saw it speaking, they were willing to oppose contrary statements, whether they were from a pope, council, or a church father. But Christians disagreed about the nature of the Spirit's illumining of the Word. Thus Gregory argues that radical critics of the Magisterial Reformation agreed with its Catholic critics, rightly noting that "both recognized that *sola Scriptura*, even when supplemented by an insistence on the illuminating influence of the Holy Spirit, had created an unintended jungle of incompatible truth claims among those who rejected the Roman church, with no foreseeable likelihood of resolution."[7] Yet these radical critics could not avoid the problem of the *sola Scriptura* Protestants: "By relativizing the importance of biblical exegesis in an effort to transcend doctrinal controversies, spiritualists actually exacerbated the problem they sought to resolve."[8] Eventually rationality would be used to adjudicate between the plurality of theological claims made by *sola Scriptura* Protestants and spiritualists; yet again, discursive rationality only exacerbated the interpretive

5. Ibid., 95. But see the analysis of Karl Holl, "Luther und die Schwärmer," in Karl Holl, *Gesammelte Aufsätze zur Kirchengeschichte, Band I* (Tübingen: Mohr-Siebeck, 1923), 420–67; Mark U. Edwards, *Luther and the False Brethren* (Stanford: Stanford University Press, 1975).
6. Ibid., 95 (emphasis original).
7. Ibid., 100; see also 151–52.
8. Ibid., 101.

pluralism and, thus, the religious and intellectual divisions of modern Western society.[9]

Gregory's argument is panoramic and epic. He moves through myriad paths to argue that "the Reformation is the most important distant historical source for contemporary Western hyperpluralism with respect to truth claims about meaning, morality, values, priorities, and purpose."[10] His description of *sola Scriptura* is matched by another recent account, this one in A. N. Williams's account on "Tradition." By reading Williams in light of Gregory, we can begin to see a common assessment of *sola Scriptura* as ecclesiologically ruinous and epistemologically fatal.

Williams begins by defining *sola Scriptura*: "In theory, the Reformers' cry of *sola Scriptura!* denied any authority to tradition whatsoever, as long as it were taken to be, at least in part or in some sense, extra-biblical."[11] The claim is total: no "authority to tradition whatsoever." This is illustrated by the way that Williams believes a World Council of Churches document disproves *sola Scriptura*: citing Jaroslav Pelikan's summary of that text, she says that "theological history makes the Reformation's rejection of tradition obsolete, that theological historiography makes the Reformation's depreciation of tradition untenable, and that theological historicism makes the Reformation's affirmation of tradition impossible."[12] Clearly she believes *sola Scriptura* involves reading the Bible alone in a vacuum created by the absence of any interpretive traditions or authorities, nothing that might be labeled "tradition" or "traditional."

No less stark are her descriptions of present-day reality: "Today it is hard to find even theoretical proponents of the *sola Scriptura*

9. Ibid., 107, 112–23. The pluralism fostered by biblical study among those committed to the *sola Scriptura* principle can be seen in Paul C. H. Lim, "Platonic Captivity of Sublime Mystery? The Trinity and the Gospel of John in Early Modern England," in *Mystery Unveiled: The Crisis of the Trinity in Early Modern England*, Oxford Studies in Historical Theology (New York: Oxford University Press, 2012), 271–319 (esp. 318–19).

10. Gregory, *Unintended Reformation*, 369; cf. Jean Bethke Elshtain, *Sovereignty: God, State, and Self: The Gifford Lectures* (New York: Basic, 2008), 77–90.

11. A. N. Williams, "Tradition," in *The Oxford Handbook of Systematic Theology*, ed. John Webster, Kathryn Tanner, and Iain Torrance (New York: Oxford University Press, 2007), 364.

12. Ibid., citing the World Council of Churches Faith and Order Commission, *The Old and the New in the Church* (London: SCM, 1961), 36.

principle." This lack of contemporary affirmation is the result of a rather simple observation: "Writers from Reformation churches have increasingly acknowledged that Scripture requires interpretation, and if one takes tradition to be simply the body of interpretation of scripture acknowledged as authoritative by the church, it becomes impossible to oppose scripture and tradition as they have sometimes been in the past."[13] Reading backwards, then, she implies that *sola Scriptura* involves a denial of interpretation and/or its authoritative form in the church's tradition. She sees some recent development in these lines: "It is, however, possible to acknowledge scripture's need for interpretation and grant some degree of normative status to some of its interpreters, while still maintaining that scripture is the supreme authority, a position which is increasingly characteristic of evangelicals such as Geoffrey Bromiley."[14] Apparently some evangelicals have begun to listen to tradition and to the authoritative interpreters of the Bible to some extent, but in so doing these recent theologians are modifying or changing the nature of biblical authority when construed along the lines of *sola Scriptura*.

Common to these accounts is a narrowed focus upon the doctrine of *sola Scriptura*. Gregory and Williams share the worry that *sola Scriptura* is unfeasible. Gregory believes it unworkable inasmuch as it proves incapable of stopping the development of a wide variety of readings of the Bible. It can be manipulated and maneuvered in such a way that the church and, by extension, the Bible cannot authoritatively control doctrinal truth-claims made by all involved. Williams believes it intellectually inoperable unless one only sticks to the words of the Bible or avoids any and all engagement of extra-biblical

13. Williams, "Tradition," 365.

14. Ibid. A similar maneuver occurs in Thomas Guarino's analysis of *sola Scriptura*: while he notes that Kevin Vanhoozer and other Protestants do not mean to suggest that Scripture is the only authority, he nonetheless insists on construing *sola Scriptura* to imply such (*Vincent of Lérins and the Development of Christian Doctrine*, Foundations of Theological Exegesis and Christian Spirituality [Grand Rapids: Baker Academic, 2013], 93–96). One wishes that Gaurino might show the same sensitivity to read *sola Scriptura* in its doctrinal context as he does so admirably with regard to Vincent's canon regarding catholicity as that which is held "always, everywhere, and by everyone" in the church (which he rightly suggests must be read alongside his second canon, which addresses the validity and need for ongoing development of doctrine: see 15, 81, 86, 88).

sources (whether traditions from inside the church or outside in the culture or in the rationality of one's time and place). In place of this fated *sola Scriptura* approach, she suggests: "Perhaps the best hope for avoiding the twin traps of naïve Biblicism and dead traditionalism lies in stressing the dialogical nature of tradition: it is the ever-unfolding dialogue of scripture with the community it addresses."[15] But this is precisely what she has earlier said cannot be affirmed by anyone who touts *sola Scriptura*! *Sola Scriptura* in either case is an intellectually and ecclesially thin approach to receiving the Word of God. It involves the absence of any genuine ecclesial authority or tradition.

Two hundred years ago Alexis de Tocqueville offered a similar reading of the Protestant Reformation and its link to modern individualism and rationalism. Reflecting on his travel throughout America he observed:

In the sixteenth century reformers submitted to the judgment of individual reason some of the dogmas of the ancient faith but continued to bar discussion of all others. In the seventeenth century, Bacon in the natural sciences and Descartes in philosophy rejected received formulations, destroyed the empire of tradition, and overthrew the authority of the master. Finally, generalizing the same principle, the philosophers of the eighteenth century set out to subject all beliefs to the scrutiny of each individual. *Who does not see that Luther, Descartes, and Voltaire all employed the same method and differed only as to the breadth of applicability they claimed for it?*[16]

Tocqueville interprets the Reformational impulse as one of individual reasoning within a vacuum wherein no tradition or authority figure dictates or directs intellectual reflection. Descartes and Voltaire only extended the reach of individualism and rationalism beyond the

15. Williams, "Tradition," 376.
16. Alexis de Tocqueville, "On the Philosophical Method of the Americans," in *Democracy in America*, trans. Arthur Goldhammer (New York: Library of America, 2004), 485 (emphasis added). For a contrary assessment in Tocqueville's own century, see Philip Schaff, *The Principle of Protestantism: As Related to the Present State of the Church*, ed. Bard Thompson and George H. Bricker, trans. John W. Nevin, Lancaster Series on the Mercersburg Theology 1 (Eugene, OR: Wipf & Stock, 2004), 78–79 (pt. 1, chap. 2).

narrow confines of Luther's initial endeavors.[17] Gregory and Williams are divided with regard to this claim that the reformers intended anything like what Tocqueville describes (and assumes) regarding modern intellectual and cultural history, but they are both in agreement with his assessment in terms of actual impact. Further, they (unlike Tocqueville) find this to be terribly problematic and theologically deficient.

Shared as well among these accounts is a reduction of theological reasoning to the claim of *sola Scriptura*. In other words, Scripture is removed from its involvements with the ongoing life of the Christian community, much less the ongoing agency of the Triune God. What has led to such distance between Bible and tradition, between Scripture and the church? Why is the authority of these texts somehow viewed as an alternative to rather than a directive for engagement with the catholic tradition? We will suggest that two classic errors are evident in *sola Scriptura* as described by Gregory, Williams, and Tocqueville. We might identify these targets as a theology at once both Donatist and deist.

First, there is a Donatist shift. Remember that in the fourth and fifth centuries the Donatists believed that the church was pure, and, therefore, they opposed the return of those who had caved in to pressure during periods of persecution. They insisted that such disloyal church members could not be restored to good standing, precisely because they had a very elevated sense of the church's holiness. A Donatist tendency can be seen in purist approaches to the church's faith and practice. Here theological reflection cannot be helped by a flawed and fallen church. The church is divided, sinful, and marred by deformities. Thus, the call is to reflect critically and individually upon the practices of the church from outside those practices, rather than from within them. While Gregory notes that the catholic church never perfectly resembled the kingdom of God, this is not to say that elements of it—its essence—were not the kingdom of God as such.[18] John Webster has written of how we do well to ask if the Protestant concern for purity might lead to a failure to honor the plenitude of

17. For Voltaire's reflections on applying rational, individual assessment to all the claims of creedal orthodoxy, for example, see *Select Works of Voltaire*, ed. Joseph McCabe (London: Watts & Co., 1935), 113.

18. Gregory, *Unintended Reformation*, 84–86, 139–45.

God's self-revelation.[19] Gregory certainly describes a *sola Scriptura* Protestantism that is Donatist in style—wherein tradition can only be valid if perfectly aligned and generated by the Holy Scriptures. In so doing, zeal for biblical purity may well lead to overlooking the fullness of God's involvements in ecclesial history and even his providential and spiritual leading of an imperfect but genuine church; her traditions, creeds, liturgies, practices, and spiritual authority may be dismissed because they are not hand-delivered in immaculate and resplendent glory.

Second, the modern era also births a deistic approach. Here theological practice is entirely and exclusively human activity with divine agency bracketed off to the past. Mark Bowald has argued that "most contemporary accounts of biblical hermeneutics are deistic."[20] Nothing remains but a divine deposit left for the pious Christian or, perhaps, the objective scholar, to unearth and appreciate. The involvement of God is entirely described in the past tense: God did reveal, God did speak, God did give us an inscripturated Word. The present tense is entirely immanent, however, and involves only our own activities: receiving, reading, studying, questioning, critiquing, and so on. Method becomes important—whether historical or practical, hermeneutical or rhetorical. Because God is presumed not to be involved in the present horizon of communication, everything hangs on negotiating the text wisely and objectively. Gregory and Williams portray *sola Scriptura* Protestantism as elevating the role of the scholar or the especially pious person—in either case, one who can access the true meaning of the text (whether historically or spiritually) just as well as any ecclesiastical authority or council.

According to these accounts, then, *sola Scriptura* characterizes Protestant ecclesiology and epistemology as tradition-less and individualistic. Further, we can see that it paints a portrait that tends toward the Donatist and deist errors, suggesting that the church is

19. John Webster, "Purity and Plenitude: Evangelical Reflections on Congar's Tradition and Traditions," *International Journal of Systematic Theology* 7, no. 4 (2005): 402.

20. Mark Bowald, *Rendering the Word in Theological Hermeneutics: Mapping Divine and Human Agency* (Aldershot, UK: Ashgate, 2007), 173. For further criticism of deistic approaches to biblical interpretation, see Herman Bavinck, *Reformed Dogmatics*, vol. 1, *Prolegomena*, ed. John Bolt, trans. John Vriend (Grand Rapids: Baker Academic, 2003), 384–85.

only of use when perfect and that the process of theological reflection is an exclusively human or natural affair. *Sola Scriptura* represents a break from that catholic tradition and from the fullness of the grace given by the Triune God. In this portrait, to affirm this reform regarding biblical authority means to distance oneself or place oneself at odds with the catholic church and the divine economy of which it has been a part and instead to place oneself within a natural economy of individual rational activity regarding God's actions long ago in a land far away.

The Churchly Context for Triune Speech

One does well to ask, Do Gregory and Williams portray *sola Scriptura* in its traditional form? Do they portray it in its best form? Do they portray it in a biblical form? If they do, and if their critiques are necessary objections, then one is hard-pressed to continue affirming such a doctrine. But if they do not account for the wisest, most faithful forms of this doctrine, then one need not view their objections as besetting.[21] If their account is not supported by the key sources, then perhaps *sola Scriptura* need not be viewed as a departure from catholicity but as an entailment of catholicity itself.

The key issue is to ask the following question: do classical adherents of *sola Scriptura* teach and practice a minimalist account of divine agency and an individualist form of Christian theology? The late Scottish theologian T. F. Torrance addressed the question of the Bible's place in the project of divine self-revelation. His reflections may give shape to our own inquiry.

> The source of all our knowledge of God is his revelation of himself. We do not know God against his will, or behind his back, as it were, but in accordance with the way in which he has elected to disclose

21. At least one recent analysis by a Roman Catholic theologian portrays *sola Scriptura* in a very different vein, so much so that he believes it might even be embraced, in a qualified way, by Roman Catholics; see Benedict Thomas Viviano, "The Normativity of Scripture and Tradition in Recent Catholic Theology," in *Scripture's Doctrine and Theology's Bible: How the New Testament Shapes Christian Dogmatics*, ed. Markus Bockmuehl and Alan Torrance (Grand Rapids: Eerdmans, 2008), 139–40.

himself and communicate his truth in the historical-theological context of the worshipping people of God, the Church of the Old and New Covenants. That is the immediate empirical fact with which the Holy Scriptures of the Old and New Testaments are bound up.[22]

Torrance addresses what he terms "the immediate empirical fact" of Holy Scripture. He does not remove Scripture from concrete situations of historical life. But he does broaden the horizons of such description by pointing beyond mere sociological inquiry or political characterization to address the redemptive-historical and self-revelatory action of the Triune God: the "worshipping people of God, the Church of the Old and New Covenants" is the space within which God is known via Holy Scripture. Scripture is the final source and authority for knowing God, but there is a catholic shape and context that involves the fullness of the church's life as the matrix within which the Scriptures are read and received. The worship of the people of God is the way in which the Bible is present to the church, as Scripture is prayed, sung, read, preached, and sacramentally practiced.

This description of divine self-revelation occurs in a study of patristic hermeneutics. Torrance—so frequently driven by the early, ecumenical theology of the fourth century—reflects on the interpretative practices of Athanasius, the Cappadocians, and Augustine here. Might the Reformation and its insistence on *sola Scriptura* render such a catholic heritage unstable or unfeasible? Can the heirs of Luther, Zwingli, Calvin, and the rest of their reforming cohort affirm these claims of Torrance? We do well to examine the writings of the Reformation to see if they illustrate an approach similar to that described by Gregory and Williams or one more in line with that presented by Torrance. In other words, we shall read the Reformation texts on scriptural authority with an interest in linking them to the catholic consensus of the patristic era and with a question regarding their relationship to modern individualism. In what ways is *sola Scriptura* orthodox? In what way might it be modern? As we survey the texts of the early Reformed movement, we see that the *sola Scriptura* principle is meant to shape engagement of the catholic tradition rather than to

22. T. F. Torrance, *Divine Meaning: Studies in Patristic Hermeneutics* (Edinburgh: T&T Clark, 1995), 5.

exclude it.[23] We will consider one influential treatise, Martin Bucer's
On the Kingdom of Christ (De Regno Christi), as well as the witness
of the early Reformed confessions regarding the catholic context of
the Protestant *sola Scriptura* principle. Then we will turn to appreciate
three practices of the early Reformational movement, each of which
locates *sola Scriptura* amid a wider catholic context.

Martin Bucer: The Kingdom of Christ and the Kings of This Age

Martin Bucer, the great reformer of Strasbourg and mentor to John
Calvin, wrote his volume *On the Kingdom of Christ (De Regno
Christi)* to address issues of Christology and authority. Penned for
Edward VI, the king of England, upon Bucer's arrival in that country, the treatise addresses the ways in which the reign of an earthly
lord might honor the kingdom of the Only Wise Sovereign. Indeed
Bucer's treatise manifests a concern that the monarch exercise genuine
spiritual authority. But, in turning to matters ecclesiastical and civil,
Bucer's approach can only be called christological. While he does
proceed to address some fourteen areas of legal formation of a society
that honors Christ, he does so in the wake of affirming the ongoing
agency of the risen Christ. His descriptions of biblical authority (or
any other sort: whether pastoral or regal) must be contextualized
within the economy of the gospel. Indeed his political program is
only articulated at any length upon reflection of biblical prophecy,
wherein the Triune God pledges to shed abroad the knowledge of
God in Christ.[24] Certain principles and policies are set forth, precisely
because they enable us to participate in the ways in which the risen
Jesus promises to be present and to communicate his lordship.

To begin, we ought to observe a similarity and a difference between
the kingdoms of this world and the kingdom of Christ. First, both

23. For further historical analysis in this regard, see Susan E. Schreiner, *Are You
Alone Wise? The Search for Certainty in the Modern Era*, Oxford Studies in Historical
Theology (New York: Oxford University Press, 2011), 80–83.
24. See especially Martin Bucer, *De Regno Christi*, in *Melanchthon and Bucer*, ed.
Wilhelm Pauck, Library of Christian Classics (Louisville: Westminster John Knox,
2006), 192–207 (chap. 3).

realms are ruled by a single person. Each realm is ruled by a single monarch, whether Edward VI or Jesus Christ. Second, the earthly realm requires representatives or stand-ins precisely because that single ruler cannot be present everywhere; yet this does not carry over to the spiritual kingdom, for Christ is everywhere. "But our heavenly King, Jesus Christ, is, according to his promise, with us everywhere and every day, 'to the consummation of the world' (Matt. 28:20). He himself sees, attends to, and accomplishes whatever pertains to the salvation of his own. Therefore he has no need of representatives to take his place."[25] Still later: "He rules and governs those who have been incorporated into himself and his Church. . . . He also shapes and perfects them, using for this purpose the ministry of his word and sacraments through fitting ministers."[26] Bucer seems to affirm that Christ is everywhere ruling, yet he is sometimes employing an intermediary or ambassador.[27]

Bucer insists that Christ does desire his followers to make use of earthly means of grace. Christ's concern is the salvation of his people and the worship of God. Yet "whatever does not contribute to this end, and nothing can do so which has not been ordained for this purpose by the Son of God and so commended to us, should be rejected and abolished by those who wish the Kingdom of Christ restored among them: such as, for example, all dogmas of religion not derived from Holy Scripture."[28] Bucer speaks of ministers and pastors as "ordained" and "appointed." Their authority is created, given, and derived from that of Christ.[29]

Thus Bucer characterizes earthly lords as "ministers" and their labor as "administrative."

The Kingdom of our Savior Jesus Christ is that administration and care of the eternal life of God's elect, by which this very Lord and King of

25. Ibid., 179–80 (chap. 2).

26. Ibid., 225.

27. Reflections on concursus surely go some way to making sense of this seeming paradox (see ibid., 185, 241). For reflection on Bucer's doctrine of concursus as well as primary and secondary causality, see Brian Lugioyo, Martin Bucer's *Doctrine of Justification: Reformation Theology and Early Modern Irenicism*, Oxford Studies in Historical Theology (New York: Oxford University Press, 2010), 99.

28. Bucer, *De Regno Christi*, 226.

29. Ibid., 182; see also 199.

Heaven by his doctrine and discipline, administered by suitable ministers chosen for this very purpose, gathers to himself his elect, those
dispersed throughout the world who are his but whom he nonetheless
wills to be subject to the powers of the world.[30]

These terms "minister" and "administration" are inherently subordinate. A minister is one who serves the *magister* or lord. More
pointedly, a minister takes the directive of the *magister* and brings it
to manifestation. Ministers do not create policy on their own; such
would be a political coup. A minister only administers that which has
been mandated by the lord. But in the administration of the lord's
will the minister does function as the lord's *magisterium*. So Bucer
insists: "It is necessary that those who are warned and corrected by
their brethren according to the Lord's precept should acknowledge
and accept in them the authority and *magisterium* of Christ himself
and gratefully and earnestly receive and follow this kind of admoni-
tion and correction as becomes good disciples of Christ."[31] He then
says that despising the minister who admonishes them is equivalent to
spurning Christ himself, while paying attention to devout correction
or encouragement is identical to hearing Christ's voice.

Indeed the preaching of the Word of God is itself heard as the
Word of God. "For true kings, who are none other than Christians,
know that they hear Christ when they hear his true ministers, and
that they reject Christ when they despise them (Luke 10:16). For the
Lord sends his ministers as the Father has sent him (John 20:21)."
Indeed, "when the ministers of the churches have been legitimately
established and they rightly fulfill their office, all true kings and
princes humbly hear the voice of Christ from the ministers and respect in them the majesty of the Son of God, as they administer not
their own but only the words and mysteries of Christ, the words and
mysteries of eternal life."[32]

30. Ibid., 225; see also 241–42.
31. Ibid., 241.
32. Ibid., 187, 188. The rightful fulfillment of legitimate office is perhaps most
blatantly found in Bucer's exegesis of Matt. 18:15–20, wherein he argues that churchly
discipline bears Christ's authority "gravely" to bind and to loose in heaven the things
of earth.

Bucer affirms biblical authority, and he subordinates all other dispensations underneath the rule of scriptural authority. "All doctrine must be derived from Holy Scriptures. It is not permissible to add or subtract anything (Deut. 4:2 and 12:32)."[33] He will unpack the "periods of the church" and note ways in which various epochs involved usurpation of divine authority by adding to or subtracting from the mandate of Holy Scripture.[34] Yet Bucer goes on to express the way in which biblical authority is "manifested" to Christians in a host of ways. He identifies the reading of Scripture—its interpretation—by "the sound teaching of religion," "by pious exhortations, admonitions, reproofs, and testimonials taken from the same Scriptures," "by the religious instruction of the ignorant" and "repetition of what has been heard from the doctrine of Christ," "by holy conversations and disputations" that address difficulties or misunderstandings, and "also by private teaching, exhortation, consolation, and correction."[35] He then presses on to address the "useful" and "even necessary" nature of catechizing the "more unlearned," likening this practice to the necessary guidance of a teacher who would never think it enough to recommend good reading apart from guiding, questioning, and reviewing the material with the students.[36]

Bucer's vision of authority can be summed up. Christ is Lord, and the Risen One exercises his rule everywhere. In sovereign rule, he ordains and appoints earthly ministers to serve as signs and instruments of his authority. The ultimate earthly sign, of course, is his Holy Scripture, which must authorize all other signs. Indeed, Holy Scripture provides the warrant and mandate for all other ministerial projects: be they homiletical, sacramental, catechetical, or disciplinary. Bucer clearly affirms *sola Scriptura*, but he uses this doctrine to engage more deeply the catholic fullness of the church's past rather than to hold tradition at bay, to avoid the diverse forms of ecclesial formation, or to nullify ecclesiastical authority.

33. Bucer, *De Regno Christi*, 232.
34. Ibid., 202–24 (chap. 4).
35. Ibid., 233. Later Bucer will speak of "administering" doctrine as a synonymous term to ways in which biblical teaching is "manifested" (see 236).
36. Ibid., 234.

The Early Reformed Confessions: Scripture and Tradition

The confessions of the sixteenth-century Reformed churches demonstrate that Bucer's theological approach is not anachronistic. Indeed, it is worth noting that Bucer's description of biblical authority within the matrix of God's speech in and to the church fits with the catholic character of the early Reformed confessions. Sometimes Bucer is viewed as irenic to a fault, too keen to show familiarity with or dependence upon the catholic tradition. But in this arena Bucer's argument is standard fare. To show its Reformational pedigree, we will survey the teaching of a number of sixteenth-century Reformed confessions and show the way in which they contextualize *sola Scriptura* among other teachings and practices of ecclesial authority.[37]

The Holy Scriptures are authoritative. Indeed, the Holy Scriptures are the gold standard of Christian authorities in the creaturely realm. The 1559 French Confession of Faith portrays the role of *sola Scriptura* in the life of the church:

> Inasmuch as it is the rule of all truth, containing all that is necessary for the service of God and for our salvation, it is not lawful for men, nor even for angels, to add to it, to take away from it, or to change it. Whence it follows that no authority, whether of antiquity, or custom, or numbers, or human wisdom, or judgments, or proclamations, or edicts, or decrees, or councils, or visions, or miracles, should be opposed to these Holy Scriptures, but, on the contrary, all things should be examined, regulated, and reformed according to them.[38]

This confession addresses a variety of potential authorities—"whether of antiquity, or custom, or numbers, or human wisdom,

---

37. One could move in the other direction, of course, by considering the way in which Bucer's project is picked up by Reformed theologians in the period of Protestant Orthodoxy; for example, see an illuminating account of this interplay of Scripture and tradition in the dogmatics of Francis Turretin in Henk van den Belt, *The Authority of Scripture in Reformed Theology: Truth and Trust*, Studies in Reformed Theology 17 (Leiden: Brill, 2008), 156–58, 163.

38. "The French Confession of Faith (1559)," in *Reformed Confessions of the Sixteenth Century*, ed. Arthur C. Cochrane (Louisville: Westminster John Knox, 2003), 145–46 (art. 5). See also "The Geneva Confession (1536)," in *Reformed Confessions*, 120 (chap. 1).

or judgments, or proclamations, or edicts, or decrees, or councils, or visions, or miracles"—and refers each one back to Scripture as its corroborating warrant. All Christian experience, ranging from the political to the pneumatic, should be "examined" by the Scriptures. As it unpacks the notion of examination, the confession goes on to speak of being "regulated" and "reformed according to them," clearly manifesting the ultimate authority of the written Word.

The confessions point to the self-attestation of Scripture as the way in which its authority makes itself apparent to us. The 1559 French Confession of Faith also manifests this concern: "We believe that the Word contained in these books has proceeded from God, and receives its authority from him alone, and not from men."[39] Here the polemical intent is to deny the notion that the church gives or even makes plain the Bible's authority. The authority and attestation of the Scriptures is a divine right, not a human bestowal.

In limiting tradition as an authority, the confessions nonetheless insist on its role in shaping faith and practice. "The Church of Christ makes no laws or commandments without God's Word. Hence all human traditions, which are called ecclesiastical commandments, are binding upon us only in so far as they are based on and commanded by God's Word."[40] Here the second of the Ten Theses of Berne addresses a broad category of "human traditions," which do carry authority yet "only in so far as they are based on and commanded by" the Holy Scriptures.[41] Indeed, this term becomes a technical term by the confessions and the early Reformed dogmatic tradition: "human traditions" are those ecclesiastical developments that purport to carry churchly authority yet lack biblical warrant.[42] For example, Zwingli's Sixty-Seven Articles of 1523 says that "in the Gospel we learn that human doctrines and traditions are of no avail to salvation"; and the First Helvetic Confession of 1536 says that "we regard all other human doctrines and articles which lead us away from God and true faith as

---

39. "The French Confession of Faith (1559)," in *Reformed Confessions*, 145 (art. 5).

40. "The Ten Theses of Berne (1528)," in *Reformed Confessions*, 49 (thesis 2).

41. The terminology of "human traditions" or "the commandments of men" derives from Matt. 15:9.

42. "Human traditions" are juxtaposed with "divine traditions" in this technical terminology (see "The Tetrapolitan Confession [1530]," in *Reformed Confessions*, 71–72 [chap. 14]).

vain and ineffectual"; and the Geneva Confession of 1536 says that "all laws and regulations made binding on conscience which oblige the faithful to things not commanded by God, or establish another service of God than that which he demands," are human traditions and "perverse doctrines of Satan."[43] In all these contexts the notion of merely human traditions are in play. But the confession of Berne in 1528 uses the term "human traditions" in a neutral way, noting that some "human traditions" do carry biblical warrant and, thus, genuine ecclesial authority, while others lack such grounding in the Scriptures. All, however, are subordinate to biblical tradition.

Still further, in qualifying the authority of ministers, the confessions attest their genuine responsibility and rule in the church. Therefore, the Scots Confession of 1560 suggests that we neither "rashly condemn" nor "receive uncritically" what is done in lawful assembly of church leaders.[44] Leadership in its various veins is to be received without either rash condemnation or uncritical reflection. Pastoral authority is genuine yet subordinated to the biblical authorization of ministerial office. Precisely this concern leads to the development of a burgeoning literature on "Christian liberty" and the way in which pastors may only bind the conscience of the Christian when Holy Scripture so binds, through its clear warrant or by good and necessary inference. The Westminster Confession of Faith, penned in the mid-seventeenth century, offers the most developed attestation to this deep Reformed concern.[45] Pastors are not given *carte blanche* authority to enforce whatever whim they might have; their authority can only be employed to teach and enforce biblical faith and practice. The confessions surely agree with Heinrich Bullinger's assessment: "Canonical truth teaches us that Christ himself holds and exercises absolute or full power in the Church, and that he has given ministerial

43. "Zwingli's Sixty-Seven Articles (1523)," in *Reformed Confessions*, 37 (art. 17); "The First Helvetic Confession (1536)," in *Reformed Confessions*, 101 (chap. 4); and "The Geneva Confession (1536)," in *Reformed Confessions*, 124 (chap. 17).
    44. "The Scots Confession (1560)," in *Reformed Confessions*, 178 (chap. 20).
    45. "The Westminster Confession of Faith (1646)," in *Creeds of the Churches: A Reader in Christian Doctrine from the Bible to the Present*, ed. John H. Leith, 3rd ed. (Atlanta: John Knox, 1982), 215–16 (chap. 20). For reflection on Christian liberty in areas of the church's engagement with politics, see Michael Allen, *Reformed Theology* (London: T&T Clark, 2010), 169–77.

power to the Church, which executes it for the most part by ministers, and religiously executes it according to the rule of God's Word."[46] Indeed the Geneva Confession of 1536 speaks similarly: "To these [ministers of the Word] we accord no other power or authority but to conduct, rule, and govern the people of God committed to them by the same Word, in which they have power to command, defend, promise, and warn, and without which they neither can nor ought to attempt anything."[47]

Ultimately, the confessions point to the continuing agency of the Risen One, who speaks through his inscripturated Word and illumines its reading, preaching, and enactment by his Holy Spirit. Thus the confessions receive the pastoral witness of the catholic past with gratitude and thanks: "Where the holy fathers and early teachers, who have explained and expounded the Scripture, have not departed from this rule, we want to recognize and consider them not only as expositors of Scripture, but as elect instruments through whom God has spoken and operated."[48] Such receptivity of the catholic tradition is neither uncritical nor rashly condemning: it is a posture of biblical dependence upon the testimony of the Spirit's work through the communion of saints and, more specifically, their authorized ministers.

Reformational Practices: Catholic and Reformed

The practices of the Reformational churches bear out this posture of biblical dependence. In various ways, they lived a Christianity that was gathered around the Holy Scriptures but inclusive of a host of practices or traditions that were meant to shape wise reading and faithful living before God. Of course, the very existence of confessional writings is a sign of genuine ecclesial authority. These documents give public attestation to the church's hearing of the gospel and to its testimony before others. More specifically, these texts bind the church's ministry to public standards and, in so doing, authorize a particular sort of

46. Heinrich Bullinger, "Of the Holy Catholic Church," in *Zwingli and Bullinger*, ed. G. W. Bromiley, Library of Christian Classics (Louisville: Westminster John Knox, 2006), 324.

47. "The Geneva Confession (1536)," in *Reformed Confessions*, 125–26 (chap. 20).

48. "The First Helvetic Confession (1536)," in *Reformed Confessions*, 101 (chap. 3).

engagement with the biblical writings. While the Reformed confessions root their claims in the ultimate authority of Scripture alone, they bear witness to and themselves manifest a catholic context for the hearing of and testimony to the Word of God in Holy Scripture.

The Reformational practice of discipleship also attests to the catholic context of biblical authority. Zacharias Ursinus left us a wonderful commentary on the Heidelberg Catechism. In the "general prolegomena" to that commentary, he addressed the question: "What are the various methods of teaching and learning the doctrine of the church?" His answer was threefold. First, he argues that members learn "the system of catechetical instruction, or that method which comprises a brief summary and simple exposition of the principal doctrines of the Christian religion."[49] Second, he enjoins them to the "consideration and discussion of subjects of a general and more difficult character, or the Common Places, as they are called, which contain a more lengthy explanation of every single point, and of difficult questions with their definitions, divisions, and arguments."[50] Patristic writings are valued most highly in this second category.[51] Third, he points them to "the careful and diligent reading of the Scriptures or sacred text," which he terms "the highest method in the study of the doctrine of the church."[52] Ursinus envisions biblical study within the context of catechetical instruction and, still further, what we would now call the exposition of a systematic theology. The Bible is the "highest method in the study of the doctrine of the church," precisely because it contains the oracles of God; yet it is not to be engaged apart from the teaching instruments of Christ's church.

Perhaps a third example will connect the confessional and catechetical traditions to lived experience in a more overt way. The Reformation

---

49. Zacharias Ursinus, *Commentary on the Heidelberg Catechism*, trans. G. W. Williard (Phillipsburg, NJ: Presbyterian & Reformed, 1985), 9.

50. John Calvin's *Institutes of the Christian Religion* would surely be the most notable instance of the second occasion of theological study, a volume intended as both an extension of basic catechesis and a preparation for reading Holy Scripture.

51. For analysis of the ways in which the early Reformed theologians engaged patristic writings, see Irena Backus, *Historical Method and Confessional Identity in the Era of the Reformation, 1378–1615* (Leiden: Brill, 2003), 193–242; Scott H. Hendrix, *Tradition and Authority in the Reformation* (Aldershot, UK: Variorum, 1966), 55–68.

52. Ursinus, *Commentary on the Heidelberg Catechism*, 10.

involved, first and foremost, a concern to purify and reform the Christian liturgy in ways that conformed more precisely to biblical teaching. Invariably, Protestant cities made liturgical reform the first of their reforming acts. The Reformed churches did not suffer any lack of zeal for liturgy when compared with Rome—they simply disagreed regarding the way in which liturgical tradition should be shaped and the eventual forms that were acceptable. Whereas Rome believed that liturgical forms might be mandated by the magisterium *or* by the Scriptures, the Reformed churches insisted that every element be authorized by the Bible itself. This commitment has been known ever since as the "regulative principle."[53] In light of this principle, the Reformed churches swept certain practices out of the liturgical routine of their congregations: for example, confession, penance, and absolution given in the confessional booth prior to Eucharistic reception.[54] They did so when they found the elements lacking biblical warrant, thus demonstrating the Bible to be the ultimate authority for faith *and practice*. Yet in so doing, they really did pass on liturgical traditions or patterns to be followed by the generations to come. Biblical authority for Christian liturgical practice did not eventuate in "free worship," wherein there was no pattern for expressions of worship. Rather biblical authority—*sola Scriptura*—meant that the churches of the Reformed confession passed on liturgical patterns that were ultimately directed by Holy Scripture.

53. Invariably this principle has always involved the necessity of distinguishing between elements and forms (and sometimes even between forms and circumstances). For instance, while the Bible mandates the element of Scripture readings in worship, it does not mandate the form of that reading (whether one verse or four chapters, from Deuteronomy or from the Gospel according to Matthew, etc.). The "regulative principle" refers to elements, which necessarily take form in various circumstances according to pastoral prudence and Christian wisdom. Hence "biblical worship" in the Reformed tradition is not a homogeneous ideal but a common commitment to worship via Word, Sacrament, and Prayer that can take various contextual forms as appropriately discerned by ecclesial authorities.

54. This parallels other moves made to give due attention to the "priesthood of all believers"—the notion that spiritual growth was the calling and responsibility of all believers, not merely of a clerical class. As Matthew Myer Boulton has shown, John Calvin did not so much oppose monasticism as he intended to refine it and universalize it, so that it was practiced by all Christians—men and women, adults and children, clerics and laity—in every facet of life (*Life in God: John Calvin, Practical Formation, and the Future of Protestant Theology* [Grand Rapids: Eerdmans, 2011], pt. 1).

Study of Reformation texts renders inoperative the supposed portrait of the Reformational doctrine of *sola Scriptura* as described by Brad Gregory, A. N. Williams, and others. Far from undergirding an individualistic or biblicistic portrayal of Christianity, *sola Scriptura* operated within a catholic context that shaped the confessional, catechetical, and liturgical life of the early Reformed churches.[55] In various ways, then, the Reformed churches of the sixteenth century lived out their commitment to *sola Scriptura* in a catholic context. The Bible grounded their doctrinal confession, undergirded their pedagogical practice, and authorized their liturgical forms. But the Bible did so by generating confessional authorities, inspiring catechetical and theological disciplines, and shaping patterns of worship that were passed from one generation to another. Principled commitment to biblical authority as the ultimate determining factor for all faith and practice did not lead to diminishing concern for ecclesial authority or waning reception of church traditions. Rather *sola Scriptura* aided the course of such reception: retrieving the fullness of the catholic past while cognizant of the ever-present need for ongoing reform.

---

55. Schaff, *Principle of Protestantism*, 79 (pt. 1, chap. 2): "In order that the Scriptures may be taken as the exclusive source and measure of Christian truth, it is necessary that the faith in Christ of which they testify should be already at hand, that their contents should have been made to live in the heart by the power of the Holy Spirit accompanying the word and the church. And so all turns upon the particular constitution of this faith."

3

Retrieving *Sola Scriptura*, Part Two

Biblical Traditioning

Sola Scriptura has been accused of fostering individualism and, thus, of festering a divisive interpretive pluralism. But we have investigated the sources of Reformation theology and found these charges wanting. Martin Bucer and the theology of the Reformed confessions suggest a more expansive understanding of *sola Scriptura*, one in which biblical authority is located amid the triune economy of grace as it inaugurates a communion of saints.[1] Further, the lived theology of the Reformed churches demonstrated a commitment to *sola Scriptura* amid a concern to embrace the catholic faith and practice of Christ's church. This contextualization of *sola Scriptura* was apparent in the confessional, pedagogical, and liturgical practices of the early Reformed churches. But a question must arise: In making such claims, are the Reformed confessions and churches not stopping half-short? Are they perhaps failing to take their principal

---

1. For further explanation of the triune economy of grace, see below, "Guarding the Good Deposit: Dogmatic Tools for Thinking Scripture and Tradition Together."

impulses to their theological end? Here we must take the teaching of our Reformed forebears regarding biblical authority and its relationship to churchly tradition and look at its own biblical pedigree. Can a biblical case be made for locating the Bible alone as a final authority amid a catholic context of other, subordinate authorities in the church's life?

Psalm 145 and the Task of Testimony, Theology, and Tradition

Perhaps it is instructive to consider Psalm 145 as we begin this endeavor. This praise song "of David" pledges worship and adoration to the LORD, his "God and King" (Ps. 145:1). Not only does the psalmist pledge praise, but he promises to reflect thoughtfully upon that which is worthy of such exaltation. "On the glorious splendor of your majesty, and on your wondrous works, I will meditate" (Ps. 145:5). This twofold consideration—God's being and God's deeds—then resounds into his praise and testimony: "They shall speak of the might of your awesome deeds, and I will declare your greatness" (Ps. 145:6).[2] This psalm, then, centers upon the primary callings of God's people: proclamation and praise, witness and worship. Along the way it also locates the discipline of theology, under the guise of "meditation," as an instrument serving Christian testimony.

Psalm 145 not only outlines the call to praise the LORD and the place of theology in aiding this calling, but it also manifests the ways in which one is made ready to do so. First, it is crucial to see that Scripture guides praise. In fact, this is demonstrably so, for the instances of praise within the psalm itself are quotations of the Pentateuch. Specifically, when the psalmist's promise to someday praise turns to active praise, he makes reference to Exodus 34:6–7. "The LORD is

2. Knowledge of God also includes knowledge of ourselves, even of the entire creation, according to Psalm 145. "They shall speak of the glory of your kingdom and tell of your power, to make known to the children of man your mighty deeds, and the glorious splendor of your kingdom" (vv. 11–12). The life of God is bound up with his fellowship with humans: the kingdom of God. But all other things are known with regard to God.

gracious and merciful, slow to anger and abounding in steadfast love" (Ps. 145:8). Clearly the law of the LORD binds the adoration voiced by King David. In this case God himself guides the way that David addresses him, for this quotation comes not only from the divine Scriptures, but from the law; not only from the law but from the book of the covenant; not only from the book of the covenant but from God's own self-manifestation upon Mt. Sinai before his servant Moses. Evident in David's praise is deference to God's direction for piety and worship.

Second, the psalmist points to the witness of an ongoing interpretative community. Knowledge of the LORD is mediated by testimony; hence the importance of the claim that "one generation shall commend your works to another, and shall declare your mighty acts" (Ps. 145:4). The knowledge of God is bound up with past events, particular actions in a linear story, and so others must be told about that story. This really does happen, though, for "they shall speak of the might of your awesome deeds, and I will declare your greatness" (Ps. 145:6). "They ["all your saints" from the preceding v. 10] shall speak of the glory of your kingdom and tell of your power, to make known to the children of man . . ." (Ps. 145:11–12).[3] The psalmist was not there atop Sinai with Moses, and the psalmist was not there at the Red Sea or the Jordan River or the wall of Jericho. The psalmist lives by the testimony of his forebears and from the confessed memory of his ancestors.

The psalm, of course, does not describe a methodology or epistemology per se, but it does manifest a spiritual vitality that takes scriptural and ecclesial formation. The self-reflection of David shows the way in which God has brought him to the point of knowing and praising God: the very words of God have shaped his speech, while the people of God have testified to him of the King's mercy and goodness. His theological reflection upon his missional calling takes scriptural and traditional shape: he listens to God's own speech, and he leans upon the witness of his ancestors. And he, in turn, commits himself to passing along the divine name to others.

---

3. Throughout the Bible, we see that God's works are performed explicitly for the sake of giving knowledge of God (see, e.g., Exod. 6:7; 7:5, 17; 8:10, 22; 9:14, 29–30; 10:2; 14:4, 18; 16:12; Isa. 49:23, 26; 60:16).

The Jerusalem Council

We should not be surprised that similar spiritual dynamics are in play in the times of the apostles. If we consider the New Testament writings, we see that the Scriptures still serve as the baseline and binding authority for faith and practice, that is, not only for our thinking and reflecting but for our praising and confessing. Yet we see that the Scriptures do not speak to individual men and women in isolation but as members of a body being built up by various ministers who administer the Word to one another. Indeed, the apostolic writings also point to the present reality of an interpretative tradition that is to be preserved and passed along generation to generation. The Acts of the Apostles gives testimony to the first ecumenical council. In Acts 15 we read of the Jerusalem Council, wherein the issue of gentile converts is addressed.

In recent years the Jerusalem Council has been referenced as a paradigm for authoritative decision making in the church. Biblical scholars such as Luke Timothy Johnson, Stephen Fowl, and Sylvia Keesmaat have suggested that the ecumenical council provides a pattern for later ecclesial decisions in that it weighs not only Scripture but also spiritual experience as distinct authorities.[4] With Johnson, Fowl, and Keesmaat, we agree that the Jerusalem Council not only serves to offer a singular judgment in redemptive history regarding the influx of gentile believers into the church but also functions to provide a paradigmatic model of ecclesial authority exercised in the form of a church council.[5] The point of Acts 15 is not overtly to teach

4. Luke Timothy Johnson, *Scripture and Discernment: Decision-Making in the Church* (Nashville: Abingdon, 1996), 61–108; Stephen Fowl, *Engaging Scripture: A Model for Theological Interpretation*, Challenges in Contemporary Theology (Malden, MA: Blackwell, 1998), 101–27; Sylvia Keesmaat, "Welcoming in the Gentiles: A Biblical Model for Decision Making," in *Living Together in the Church: Including Our Differences*, ed. Greig Dunn and Chris Ambidge (Toronto: Anglican Book Centre, 2004), 30–49. In particular, each of these studies asserts that a similar argument for inclusion of homosexuals within the church as practicing homosexuals might be faithful to the ecclesiology and religious epistemology portrayed by the Acts of the Apostles.

5. Fowl is especially helpful here; see *Engaging Scripture*, 103–5; see also David G. Peterson, *The Acts of the Apostles*, Pillar New Testament Commentary (Grand Rapids: Eerdmans, 2009), 419n8 (where he deals with issues of historicity) and 445 (where he deals with the paradigmatic nature of the text, noting that this must be viewed amid its singular function in the structure of Acts and of redemptive history).

how decisions are made; rather, the immediate contextual point is redemptive-historical and related to the status of the gentiles indwelt by the Spirit. But in addressing this presenting issue, Acts 15 does reveal much about how ecclesial authority is to be exercised. Unfortunately, Johnson, Fowl, and Keesmaat do not portray its function in a helpful, balanced manner. We can consider both where their exposition is helpful and where it fails to follow the canonical portrait of this inaugural council.

Three things should be noted. First, the deliberation of the Jerusalem Council is prompted by spiritual experience: Peter's vision, Paul's first missionary journey, and the seeming presence of the Holy Spirit within gentile believers. At the council itself, experience is referenced (Acts 15:4, 12). Peter has offered analysis, reflecting on the testimony of Paul and Barnabas about gentile conversion: "God, who knows the heart, bore witness to them, by giving them the Holy Spirit just as he did to us, and he made no distinction between us and them, having cleansed their hearts by faith" (Acts 15:8–9). Peter's testimony has become God's witness experienced by Peter, Paul, and Barnabas.[6] Second, the decision of the council bears more than merely historical authority, inasmuch as it is superintended by the Holy Spirit. The judgment of "the apostles and the elders, with the whole church" (Acts 15:22) was characterized in this way: "it has seemed good to the Holy Spirit and to us" (Acts 15:28). The determination of the council is binding, because it is spiritually discerned and authorized. On these two points Johnson, Fowl, and Keesmaat are correct: the council considers spiritual experience, and the council offers an authoritative judgment.

But the authoritative judgment is based on more than mere spiritual experience, and in this third facet we must demur from the accounts of Johnson, Fowl, and Keesmaat. For instance, Fowl argues that James's argument carries the day not because it is James who says it, but because "it articulates for the community the sense of the Spirit's work."[7] This much is surely true: the authority of the apostle is related, ultimately, to the gravity of God himself. But it is not merely the Spirit's witness in recent experience whereby James receives warrant for this

---

6. Fowl, *Engaging Scripture*, 110.
7. Ibid., 112.

judgment. It is premised also upon that experience's conformity with
scriptural precedent.[8] When James spoke, he said: "Simeon has related how God first visited the Gentiles, to take from them a people
for his name. And with this the words of the prophets agree" (Acts
15:14–15). He then moves into quoting Amos 9:11–12 as prophetic
foretelling of what Peter, Paul, and Barnabas have confessed to now
be present reality (Acts 15:16–17). It is notable that James mentions
the experience as the baseline for conversation: he says "the words of
the prophets agree" with this narrative of gentile conversion, rather
than that the story of gentile conversion agrees with the Scriptures.
Still, the word order does not undo the link.[9]

Experience is not superseding Scripture, as has been suggested by
other accounts.[10] Scripture is seen to have pointed to its own culmina-
tion: the requirement of circumcision for membership in God's people
was only for a time but was foretold or figured to conclude eventually. "Only because the new experience of Gentile converts proved
hermeneutically illuminating of Scripture was the church, over time,
able to accept the decision to embrace Gentiles within the fellowship
of God's people."[11] Scripture interprets Scripture, in the deliberation
of the council, as Amos contextualizes the laws of the Pentateuch
within a certain (past) phase of redemptive history. While Fowl may
be right that the "plain sense" of certain texts may seem to push one
way (namely, that the Torah teaches the necessity of gentile converts
becoming or behaving as if Jewish: being circumcised, keeping dietary
law, etc.), the Jerusalem Council saw other texts (like Amos) offering a
"plain sense" that offered eschatological qualification of those earlier

8. Richard Bauckham, "James and the Jerusalem Church," in *The Book of Acts
in Its Palestinian Setting*, ed. Richard Bauckham (Grand Rapids: Eerdmans, 1995),
chap. 15.

9. Peterson, *Acts of the Apostles*, 430–32; contra Keesmaat, "Welcoming in the
Gentiles," 38.

10. See Keesmaat, "Welcoming in the Gentiles," 36, where she states that "there is
absolutely no biblical precedent for welcoming in Gentiles without being circumcised
and following Torah. The Pharisees who opposed Paul had both scripture and tradition
on their side." Later Keesmaat argues that James raises scriptural references only by
bringing in indirect texts that suit his purposes (39).

11. Richard B. Hays, "Homosexuality," in *The Moral Vision of the New Testament:
A Contemporary Introduction to New Testament Ethics* (New York: HarperCollins,
1996), 399.

texts.[12] In no case did the council or experience unilaterally reject the "plain sense" of Scripture. Because of the experience witnessed and its conformity to biblical teaching, the council renders a judgment agreeable to James's suggestion: "My judgment is that we should not trouble those of the Gentiles who turn to God" with things like circumcision and observance of the Israelite law (Acts 15:19, 28).

This third facet—the biblical authority for the ecclesial judgment made by this council—is also demonstrated in the moral guidance given. We have already seen that the restraint from giving certain moral mandates is owing to scriptural precedent, as James shows in Amos 9. We can now see that the ethical teaching that is offered is also rooted in the biblical writings of the people of God. There are debates as to the precise roots of the commands "to abstain from the things polluted by idols, and from sexual immorality, and from what has been strangled, and from blood," as James puts it, and to "abstain from what has been sacrificed to idols, and from blood, and from what has been strangled, and from sexual immorality," as the letter to Antioch has it (Acts 15:20, 29). Some argue that these commands point back to the Noahic laws given in Genesis 9.[13] Others believe they are all given to resident aliens among the Israelites, outlined in Leviticus 17:8–18:18.[14] In either case, however, they are being drawn from biblical teaching regarding the behavior of non-Israelites (either outside the covenant or coming into the covenant). In both its restraint and its requirements, then, the council looks to Scripture to shape its judgment: gentile converts are to obey as the Old Testament says they should (provided the Old Testament is read in such a way that its own eschatological prophecies about the redemptive-historical inclusion of gentiles, as gentile believers rather than as Israelites, is given due attention).

What, then, does the Jerusalem Council reveal about the authority of Scripture? It shows that Scripture is not the only authority, to be sure, inasmuch as an ecumenical council here renders an authoritative

12. Fowl, *Engaging Scripture*, 126.

13. F. F. Bruce, *The Book of the Acts*, rev. ed., New International Commentary on the New Testament (Grand Rapids: Eerdmans, 1988), 295–96.

14. Fowl argues that the commands stem from Leviticus 17–18 (*Engaging Scripture*, 113).

judgment. But it also shows the exegetically constrained nature of that judicial rendering. The council can bind the faith and practice of Christians only to the extent that one can say "with this the words of the prophets agree" (Acts 15:15).

Luther on the Church Councils

Martin Luther found the Jerusalem Council to provide a paradigmatic portrait of biblical tradition. In his 1539 text "On the Councils and the Church," he offered a survey of conciliar history beginning with an analysis of Acts 15 (68–79).[15] He then used that model of ecumenical authority exercised in a judicial mode to serve as a criterion for how later councils ought to function. As he articulates his understanding of the true church and of valid councils, it becomes apparent that he both affirms the necessity of church councils for Christ's continued governance of his church and understands genuine conciliar authority to be subservient always to the witness of Holy Scripture. In this regard Luther argues that his ecclesiology is catholic, faithful to the teaching of the fathers (he especially points to Augustine and Bernard), whereas the Roman Catholic ecclesiology of his day is divergent from this catholic tradition (25–27).

Luther addresses what may or may not be done at a council; he mentions ten things: five negative, five positive. "First, a council has no power to establish new articles of faith, even though the Holy Spirit is present" (123). "Second, a council has the power—and is also duty-bound to exercise it—to suppress and condemn new articles of faith, in accordance with Scripture and the ancient faith" (123). "Third, a council has no power to command new good works; it cannot do so, for Holy Scripture has already abundantly commanded all good works" (123). "Fourth, a council has the power—and is also duty-bound to exercise it—to condemn evil works that oppose love, according to all of Scripture and the ancient practice of the church, and to punish persons guilty of such works" (124). "Fifth, a council

15. Martin Luther, "On the Councils and the Church (1539)," in *Church and Ministry III*, ed. Eric W. Gritsch, trans. Charles M. Jacobs with Eric W. Gritsch, Luther's Works 41 (Philadelphia: Fortress, 1966). References to this work will be given parenthetically in text.

has no power to impose new ceremonies on Christians, to be observed on pain of mortal sin or at the peril of conscience—such as fast days, feast days, food, drink, garb" (130).

"Sixth, a council has the power and is bound to condemn such ceremonies in accordance with Scripture; for they are un-Christian and constitute a new idolatry or worship, which is not commanded by God, but is forbidden" (130). "Seventh, a council has no power to interfere in worldly law and government" (130). "Eighth, a council has the power and is bound to condemn such arbitrary ways or new laws, in accordance with Holy Scripture, that is, to throw the pope's decretals into the fire" (130–31). "Ninth, a council has no power to create statutes or decretals that seek nothing but tyranny . . . but it has the power and is bound to condemn this in accordance with Holy Scripture" (131). "Tenth, a council has the power to institute some ceremonies, provided, first, that they do not strengthen the bishops' tyranny; second, that they are useful and profitable to the people and show fine, orderly discipline and conduct. . . . In summary, these must and cannot be dispersed with if the church is to survive" (131).

Note that Luther does not deny the presence of the Holy Spirit, yet he maintains that the Spirit cannot be used as a supplement to but only a steward of the Word. In other words, the presence of the Spirit does not mean that there is an additional foundation for faith and practice. So "no new articles of faith" may be established, and no "new good works" may be promulgated.[16] Even in its opposition of new errors and challenges, councils may respond only inasmuch as these condemnations would be "in accordance with the Holy Scripture." Earlier he had noted that councils will need to consolidate the teaching of Scripture into other language for the sake of communicating it clearly (83), but he is steadfast in noting that determinations about doctrine and morality must always be rooted in scriptural warrants.

16. Remarkable parallels exist between Luther's argument that no "new articles" be formulated and the second canon of Vincent of Lérins's regarding healthy doctrinal development, which states that we ought to "speak newly, though never say new things" (see Thomas G. Guarino, *Vincent of Lérins and the Development of Christian Doctrine*, Foundations of Theological Exegesis and Christian Spirituality [Grand Rapids: Baker Academic, 2013], 15, 81, 86 [quoting Vincent's *Commonitorium* 22.7]).

Indeed Luther believes that the Roman Catholic Church does not really honor councils enough, evidenced by what he sees as their inconsistency in following the first ecumenical council. Whereas Acts 15 limits the moral requirements placed upon gentile converts, Luther believes that later Roman conciliar decisions have heaped many other burdens upon the laity (28–29). He thinks they have been similarly inconsistent in their obedience to later ecumenical councils. His response, however, is not to shirk conciliar authority but to wish for a new council to be convened to address the recent maladies (137–38). While he desires such a council, he does not think it likely that one will be summoned (141). Luther looks to the Bible alone as a foundation for faith and practice, but this bedrock sustains genuine ministries and legitimate ecclesiastical authorities (like the Jerusalem Council).

He locates the conciliar authority among the seven "holy possessions" of the church. In the third part of this treatise, he addresses those seven possessions where we can recognize a "Christian, holy people" as confessed in the Apostles' Creed (148–66). Councils are a key part of the ministry of the Word, the exercise of discipline, and the ministry of the ordained. Like other holy possessions, Luther sees more than merely human agency here. "These are the true seven principal parts of the great holy possession whereby the Holy Spirit effects in us a daily sanctification and vivification in Christ" (165–66). God is the primary agent in these gifts, even though they institute human practices and institutional patterns. They are instruments of sanctification, which Luther believes is sorely needed. In light of Luther's sense that the church has gone awry in his own day in so many ways, he desires sanctification and, thus, reform of the church, but he believes in its catholic shape.[17]

17. On the catholic shape of Luther's reformation, see Jaroslav Pelikan, *Obedient Rebels: Catholic Substance and Protestant Principle in Luther's Reformation* (New York: Harper & Row, 1964), 11; there is also much to be gleaned, critically, from Christoph Schwöbel, "The Creature of the Word: Recovering the Ecclesiology of the Reformers," in *On Being the Church: Essays on the Christian Community*, ed. Colin E. Gunton and Daniel W. Hardy (Edinburgh: T&T Clark, 1989), 110–55; David S. Yeago, "The Catholic Luther," in *The Catholicity of the Reformation*, ed. Carl W. Braaten and Robert W. Jenson (Grand Rapids: Eerdmans, 1996), 13–34; Reinhard Hütter, *Suffering Divine Things: Theology as Church Practice* (Grand Rapids: Eerdmans, 2000), 128–46 (here Hütter is helpful in offering a reading of Luther's

Other Apostolic Teaching on Tradition

The New Testament provides other examples of biblical traditioning, wherein Scripture is the ultimate authority amid a number of lesser yet no less divinely intended authorities meant to shape and sustain the faith and practice of the Christian community. For instance, when Paul writes to young Timothy about his pastoral charge, he does not merely urge him to follow in Paul's path but also to maintain a catholic heritage. It is no small thing that he calls Timothy to imitate him and to minister as he has (see 2 Tim. 1:8; 3:10–11); this itself shows that a mentor has genuine authority, and it manifests Paul, the apostle of freedom, willing to call Timothy to follow his authoritative example. Still more notable, however, is Paul's embrace of a wider pattern that both Timothy and he follow. "Follow the pattern of sound words that you have heard from me, in the faith and love that are in Christ Jesus. By the Holy Spirit who dwells within us, guard the good deposit entrusted to you" (2 Tim. 1:13–14; see also 1 Tim. 6:20). The deposit here, and explicitly in 1 Timothy 6:20, precedes Paul himself; he has been deposited or given this pattern just as much as has Timothy.[18] That which is to be guarded is not merely an object of study, but a particular "pattern" of words. The church and its ministers, according to Paul, are committed not simply to a common conversational space or subject, but to a particular approach in communicating and confessing it.[19] Paul not only notes this pattern

---

"On the Councils and the Church," which addresses the practice of *doctrina* and of ecclesial authority in a pathic rather than poietic manner, and yet which proves overly influenced by *communio* ecclesiology and less than attentive to the perfection of God—in his being and in his communication).

18. I. Howard Marshall with Philip H. Towner, *A Critical and Exegetical Commentary on the Pastoral Epistles*, International Critical Commentary (London: T&T Clark, 1999), 726–27; cf. 676. On Paul's gospel as related to earlier oral tradition, see Peter Stuhlmacher, "The Pauline Gospel," in *The Gospel and the Gospels*, ed. Peter Stuhlmacher, trans. John Vriend (Grand Rapids: Eerdmans, 1991), 156–66.

19. Donald Wood has registered concerns on this front about the way in which emphasis upon catholicity and the exegetical tradition too often skates lightly over the binding and authoritative nature of its primary form—the church's creeds and confessions—in the interests of promoting an ongoing space for conversation (see "Some Comments on Moral Realism and Scriptural Authority," *European Journal of Theology* 18, no. 2 [2009]: 151–53; see also Oliver J. O'Donovan, "The Moral Authority of Scripture," in *Scripture's Doctrine and Theology's Bible: How the New Testament*

of doctrine as something prescriptive—that which Timothy and he are to honor—but also as a pledge of God. I. Howard Marshall notes that in the previous verse, 2 Timothy 1:12, Paul has just insisted that the God whom he has believed is "able to guard until that Day what has been entrusted to me."[20] Paul expands on the way in which the Triune God does guard this deposit entrusted to Paul (and now also, by extension, to Timothy) by pointing to the Holy Spirit in verse 14. The Spirit guards the apostolic deposit by preserving its transmission and communication from one generation to the next (à la Psalm 145).

Some have suggested that this kind of portrayal of early Christianity might be termed "early Catholicism," a departure from the vibrant Paulinism of other New Testament writings. Without engaging that historiographic debate here, we can point to the continued emphasis in these Pastoral Epistles upon scriptural authority as the final arbiter of Christian faith and practice.[21] "All Scripture is breathed out by God, and profitable for teaching, for reproof, for correction, and for training in righteousness, that the man of God may be complete, equipped for every good work" (2 Tim. 3:16–17). Thus, Timothy is to "preach the Word" (2 Tim. 4:2). The apostle Paul here envisions a ministry that focuses upon preaching the Scriptures and yet doing so cognizant of a vibrant and ongoing interpretative tradition that serves to provide authoritative parameters for expositing those sacred Scriptures. Scripture and tradition are not mutually exclusive here—the former generates the latter, while the latter serves the former. One is reminded here of Ursinus's comments about how Scripture is meant to shape systematic theology which then informs catechesis; this is the order of being and of authority.[22] At the same

---

Shapes Christian Dogmatics, ed. Markus Bockmuehl and Alan J. Torrance [Grand Rapids: Baker Academic, 2008], 165–75). For further reflection, see chap. 4 below.

20. Marshall, *Pastoral Epistles*, 714–15.

21. It is worth noting a recent argument that, without ever focusing upon this genetic or developmental question, nonetheless puts the lie to the argument that there was a marked shift toward an "early Catholicism." It does so from the other side, however, by highlighting the traditioned or catholic nature of earlier texts rather than arguing for the ecclesiastical mildness of certain later texts. See Edith Humphrey, *Scripture and Tradition: What the Bible Really Says* (Grand Rapids: Baker Academic, 2013), 27–34, 43, 136–37.

22. See the section "Reformational Practices: Catholic and Reformed" in chap. 2 above.

time, however, the order of knowing runs precisely the other way: one is catechized, then formed as a theologian, and finally capable of reading the Bible well.

The psalms and the apostles point alike to the authority of the Scriptures and to the divine design behind the ecclesiastical context for receiving those Scriptures as our final authority for faith and practice. Whether in the self-testimony of a David or the pastoral wisdom of a Paul, biblical authority is not juxtaposed with but paired alongside thick practices of catholic traditioning. This interplay between the Bible as the ultimate authority and its authorized interpretation via ecclesiastical ministries is apparent in the first ecumenical council held in Jerusalem, according to the reports of Acts 15.

The prophetic and apostolic testimony authorizes the ministry of an evangelical tradition. So the reformers did not insist upon and manifest an ongoing commitment to traditioning practices in their Christian communities in some non- or anti-scriptural guise. Rather, their encouragement of such developments was generated by exegetical reflection on the way the Bible addresses authority, discipleship, and ministry. *They are traditional precisely because they are biblical; indeed, because they are fundamentally biblical, they are fully traditional.* Heinrich Bullinger is emblematic in this regard:

> But if the Church has received power to appoint suitable ministers for the Church, I do not think that there are any who will deny that it has the authority to depose the unworthy and wicked deceivers, and also to correct and amend those things which if they are lacking may appear to be necessary for this purpose. And since ministers are chosen chiefly to teach, it follows necessarily that the Church has power to teach, to exhort, to comfort and such like by means of its lawful ministers: yet not the power to teach everything, but only that which it received as delivered from the Lord by the doctrine of the prophets and apostles. . . . But this ministry and office of preaching is simply the power of keys received by the Church. . . . Furthermore, that the Church has power to give judgment on doctrines appears from the one sentence of the apostle Paul: "Let the prophets speak two or three, and the other judge." And St. John says: "Dearly beloved, believe not every spirit, but try the spirits, whether they are of God." But there is also a fixed order in this power to judge. For the Church does not

judge according to its own pleasure, but according to the sentence of the Holy Spirit and the order and rule of the Holy Scriptures.[23]

Bullinger grounds the apostolic ministry of the church's leaders in the explicit teaching of John and Paul. Indeed, he states that this is taught by "canonical truth" and executed "according to the rule of God's Word." He points to specific teaching found in 1 Corinthians and 1 John in making his exegetical case. In other words, biblical traditioning is generated from and guarded by the scriptural teaching itself. The Bible beckons that we read it but not all by its lonesome.

Sola Scriptura is essential, but it is not enough by way of a theological program or intellectual criterion for wise thinking. It addresses one very specific question, that is, what is the ultimate authority employed by God as an instrument for shaping Christian faith and practice? This is an important question. "Scripture's task as prophetic and apostolic witness to the divine Word can only be accomplished if it is in some sense an alien element in the church."[24] There are a host of other questions *sola Scriptura* does not address. Whether we examine Reformed history or the biblical texts themselves, we see that the written Word does not do all things directly. The Word must be mediated in various forms. The Bible itself calls for the exercise of pastoral authority, confessional authority, and what we could call ecumenical authority.

Guarding the Good Deposit: Dogmatic Tools for Thinking Scripture and Tradition Together

We have seen that the reformers, through intense study of the Bible itself as their final authority, came to believe that the Bible cannot be read by itself, for it warrants or mandates the functioning of other ecclesial authorities. *To be more biblical, then, one cannot be biblicistic. To be more biblical, one must also be engaged in the process of*

23. Heinrich Bullinger, "Of the Holy Catholic Church," in *Zwingli and Bullinger*, ed. G. W. Bromiley, Library of Christian Classics (Louisville: Westminster John Knox, 2006), 321–22, 323.

24. John Webster, "Purity and Plenitude: Evangelical Reflections on Congar's Tradition and Traditions," *International Journal of Systematic Theology* 7, no. 4 (2005): 412.

traditioning. Thus, the reformers certainly understood and intended *sola Scriptura* to shape engagement of the catholic tradition and the fullness of the riches of the church, all of which are meant to work together to form members of the body for the work of ministry.

We do well, nonetheless, to acknowledge the drift away from a lively setting of *sola Scriptura* in the redemptive economy of the Triune God and amid the life of the communion of saints. Indeed, *sola Scriptura* has served for some moderns as a banner for private judgment and against catholicity. In so doing, however, churches and Christians have turned from *sola Scriptura* to *solo Scriptura*, a bastard child nursed at the breast of modern rationalism and individualism. Even the Reformational doctrine of perspicuity has been transformed in much popular Christianity and some scholarly reflection as well to function as the theological equivalent of philosophical objectivity, namely, the belief that any honest observer can, by the use of appropriate measures, always gain the appropriate interpretation of a biblical text. Yet this is a far cry from the confession of Scripture's clarity in the early Reformed movement or even in its expression by the post-Reformation dogmatics of the Reformed churches. On top of this type of mutation, we regularly encounter uses of the doctrine of the "priesthood of all believers" that ignore or minimize the role of church officers as well as the principle of *sola Scriptura* to affirm a lived practice of "no creed but the Bible."[25] Right or not, then, many people embrace *sola Scriptura*, thinking that they are embracing individualism, anti-traditionalism, and/or rationalism. Similarly, right or not, many critique *sola Scriptura* as one or more of these three things.

Cognizant of these devolutions, then, we do well to ask not simply whether or not *sola Scriptura* is culpable but also how it can be presented in such a way in days to come that will least likely be misleading. In other words, we must defend *sola Scriptura* from misunderstanding, by noting how its misapplications render false neither its fundamental basis nor its appropriate practice. We have considered this already, historically and exegetically. But we also do well to reflect on the way in which we express *sola Scriptura*, locating it within

25. For a litany of such popular uses, see Christian Smith, *The Bible Made Impossible: Why Biblicism Is Not a Truly Evangelical Reading of Scripture* (Grand Rapids: Brazos, 2012), pt. 1 (esp. chaps. 1–2).

the catholic context of God's formation of his people, so that such misunderstandings become less likely. It is one thing to affirm that the context for a doctrine of scriptural authority is the self-revelatory work of the Triune God as it takes shape amid the life of the people of God, over against the reign of hermeneutical approaches that are covertly deistic or seemingly Donatist. It is another thing to shape and sustain doctrinal concepts that point to and emphasize that link between biblical command and sovereign divine lordship amid the kingdom of the redeemed.

As we conclude this chapter, then, we will consider a few ways in which the churchly context of the Scriptures is affirmed and characterized. In each case, the link between the Bible as ultimate authority and the church as the catholic context for God's formation of his people is demonstrated and defined in some way.

Dogmatic Tool #1: The Church as the Creature of the Word

First, Reformational churches have insisted that the church is the *creature of the Word*. In this vein Paul's words to the Corinthians are vital: "For what we proclaim is not ourselves, but Jesus Christ as Lord, with ourselves as your servants for Jesus's sake. For God, who said, 'Let light shine out of darkness,' has shone in our hearts to give the light of the knowledge of the glory of God in the face of Jesus Christ" (2 Cor. 4:5–6). Paul is addressing the ministry, or *diakonian*, that he exercises (v. 1). He characterizes it as a servant role, precisely because it is created by the Word of God. The parallel or analogy, of course, is unto creation itself. God called light out of darkness, and light emerged, and it was good. Now God calls the church and her ministry out of nothing but darkness, and this witness "has shone in our hearts," and it is very good.

That the church is the creature of the Word helps avoid a faltering into a Pelagian ecclesiology. The church is brought into being from nothing by God's will and grace. "Once you were not a people, but now you are God's people"; this ecclesial creation stems from God's loving-kindness as stated next by the apostle: "Once you had not received mercy, but now you have received mercy" (1 Pet. 2:10). Peter calls the church "a chosen race" to emphasize this gracious ground of churchly reality. The church is called into being by God's electing, loving Word. Just as radically as election addresses individual salvation, so it undergirds the communal life of the people of God. It displaces the self or the society as an entity that stands due to its own action, and it replaces that myth of self-making with a narrative of God's creative agency. God has called this people into being. The election of the church leads her to sing: "The Church's one foundation is Jesus Christ, her Lord; she is his new creation by water and the Word."[26]

Lutheran theologian Carl Braaten has addressed this identification of the church as the creature of the Word and shown how it helps us think about the church in light of the gospel:

> Evangelical Protestantism is centered in the gospel. That is what the word "evangelical" means, to be defined by the evangel, the good news of the gospel. But where does the church fit in? . . . The church is the creature of the Word; the Word is prior. But in the order of human experience the church comes before the gospel. We might put it this way: in the order of being (*ordo essendi*) the gospel comes before the church, but in the order of knowledge (*ordo cognoscendi*) the church comes before the gospel. In any case, they belong together. There is no such thing as churchless Christianity, for that would posit the possibility of relating personally to Christ without being a member of his body, the church. In the New Testament and in the theology of the fathers, to be a Christian and to be a member of the body of Christ are one and the same thing.[27]

Braaten is expressing a deep catholic and Reformational commitment: that Christ is the Lord of the church, and the church is the servant of Christ. This can be expressed in various phraseologies, the head/body metaphor being only one example. In every case, however, we see that the Word creates the church, and, thus, the church confesses the Word. The gospel tells us that the God who has all life in himself shares life with us: here we see that life comes to the church by the creative Word of God, but, remarkably, this life really does come to

26. Samuel J. Stone, "The Church's One Foundation," in *Trinity Hymnal*, no. 347.
27. Carl E. Braaten, "The Problem of Authority in the Church," in *The Catholicity of the Reformation*, ed. Carl E. Braaten and Robert W. Jenson (Grand Rapids: Eerdmans, 1996), 55.

the church. She is a creature by his Word. She has life, and she has it only from this life-giving Lord.

Dogmatic Tool #2: The Church as the Hearing Church

Second, Reformational churches have testified that the church is the *hearing church*. The church lives by hearing the Word of Christ, his address and his presence to her in verbal form, wherein he exhorts and encourages and in so doing sustains her life.[28] Again the apostle Paul's reflections are generative: "Let the word of Christ dwell in you richly" (Col. 3:16). Here Paul has already addressed the high identity of God's people as "God's chosen ones, holy and beloved" (v. 12). He has also spoken at length of their high calling to be compassionate, kind, humble, meek, patient, long-suffering, forgiving, loving, and peaceful (vv. 12–15). Such an auspicious beginning (in God's creative election) and such a marvelous calling (to be that kind of moral community) raise serious questions: How could this life be sustained? Is this even possible? What means bring about such results? To these questions Paul responds with the "word of Christ" that tabernacles or rests in them richly.

The Word does not merely mark the church's beginning (as we have seen above with respect to its creation) but also maintains its being at every step of the way. "The Church is, because Jesus Christ, the Crucified and Risen One, acts upon her ever anew. . . . She was not before this action; and she is not for an instant without this action."[29] Indeed, Edmund Schlink's Reformational convictions are held deep

28. Robert Sokolowski has argued that the church speaks the Scriptures today: in other words, that "we do have a tangible and immediate speaker of the Scriptures" in the church and, by consequence, we can say that "Sacred Scripture does not exist on its own; it exists through time as spoken by the Church" (Robert Sokolowski, "God's Word and Human Speech," *Nova et Vetera* 11, no. 1 [Winter 2013]: 192). While affirming his emphasis on the churchly context for scriptural speech, Sokolowski's inflation of ecclesiology (such that the church, and not the Triune God, is the primary speaker of the Scriptures) and his ordering of Scripture vis-à-vis the church (such that the Scriptures are existent due to the church, rather than the reverse) both miss the deeper location of scriptural authority within the economy of God's continuing agency by only considering its more latent location in an ecclesial context or a churchly economy of human mediation.

29. Edmund Schlink, "Christ and the Church," in *The Coming Christ and the Coming Church* (Edinburgh: Oliver & Boyd, 1967), 116.

in the catholic tradition. One sees this in the ecclesiology of Irenaeus. "This faith which, having been received from the Church, we do pre-serve, and which always, by the Spirit of God, renewing its youth as if it were some precious deposit in an excellent vessel, causes the vessel itself containing it to renew its youth also. . . . For where the Church is, there is the Spirit of God; and where the Spirit of God is, there is the Church and every kind of grace."[30] Triune grace not only starts but sustains the life and ministry of the church. This grace comes especially in the form of the "word of Christ." This word may be administered in various ways. In Colossians 3 Paul immediately points to a variety: "teaching and admonishing one another in all wisdom, singing psalms and hymns and spiritual songs, with thankfulness in your hearts to God. And whatever you do, in word or deed, do every-thing in the name of the Lord Jesus, giving thanks to God the Father through him" (vv. 16–17). The Word is mediated by the ministry of the clergy and the laity, by spoken and sung words, by religious rites and by thankful engagement of all life's occurrences.

The Heidelberg Catechism addresses the nature of the holy, catholic church's ongoing life and sustenance: "I believe that from the begin-ning to the end of the world, and from among the whole human race, the Son of God, by his Spirit and his Word, gathers, protects, and preserves for himself, in the unity of the true faith, a congregation chosen for eternal life."[31] In recent years John Webster has offered an apt assessment: "An adequate doctrine of the church will maximize Christology and pneumatology (for it is Jesus Christ through Word and Spirit who 'gathers, protects and preserves') and relativize (but not minimize or abolish) ecclesial action and its ordered forms."[32] The church is created and cared for by the action of the Triune God. The endurance of the church is no less gracious than the election of

30. Irenaeus, "Against Heresies," in *The Apostolic Fathers with Justin Martyr and Irenaeus*, Ante-Nicene Fathers 1, ed. Alexander Roberts and James Donaldson (1956; repr., Peabody, MA: Hendrickson, 1994), 458 (3.24.1).

31. "The Heidelberg Catechism," in *Reformed Confessions of the Sixteenth Cen-tury*, ed. Arthur C. Cochrane (Louisville: Westminster John Knox, 2003), 314 (Q and A 54).

32. John Webster, "The Self-Organizing Power of the Gospel of Christ: Episcopacy and Community Formation," in *Word and Church: Essays in Christian Dogmatics* (Edinburgh: T&T Clark, 2001), 198.

God's people. The church is fed by the Word; thus, the church is a hearing church.

Dogmatic Tool #3: The Church's Ministerial Authority

Third, central not only to early Reformation-era debates but to the Reformational churches' ongoing sense of ecclesiological identity is the principle that the *church's authority is ministerial*. First Peter 2:25 tells us that there is one "overseer" or "bishop" of our souls, Jesus Christ, and yet the New Testament addresses others as overseers and bishops, *presbyters* and elders. In the Reformation era these two truths were upheld by making a distinction. Jesus Christ is the only magisterial authority in the church; the term *magister*, or lord, speaks to his final sovereignty in the church. Inasmuch as the church exercises authority, in particular through the ministry of its officers, this is a ministerial authority; the term "minister," or servant, addresses the executive function of the church's action. The officers of the church do not set principles or policy, but they administer the determinative judgments of Jesus Christ.

The apostle Paul characterizes this kind of ministry using the terminology of an ambassador in his writing to the Corinthians. Paul celebrates the grace of God: "If anyone is in Christ, he is a new creation. The old has passed away; behold, the new has come" (2 Cor. 5:17). The new creation brings not only personal salvation but also corporate shape, for Paul continues: "All this is from God, who through Christ reconciled us to himself and gave us the ministry of reconciliation" (v. 18). Paul specifies the roles. "God was reconciling the world to himself" (v. 19). Reconciliation is a divine act performed "in Christ." Yet Paul goes on to say also that God was "entrusting to us the message of reconciliation" (v. 19). He insists that the grace of God not only saves but commissions.[33] He states this in a variety of ways. In terms of identity, now "we are ambassadors for Christ." In terms of instrumentality, he can say that God is "making his ap-

---

33. Karl Barth's emphasis on vocation and witness as a crucial third aspect of soteriology, alongside justification and sanctification, affirms this Pauline reality in an especially illuminating way (see Karl Barth, *Church Dogmatics*, vol. 4, *The Doctrine of Reconciliation*, pt. 3.2, ed. G. W. Bromiley and T. F. Torrance, trans. G. W. Bromiley [Edinburgh: T&T Clark, 1961]).

peal through us." In terms of action, he says that "we implore you on behalf of Christ, be reconciled to God" (v. 20). He sums up the relationship: "Working together with him, then, we appeal to you" (2 Cor. 6:1). Paul is willing to refer to himself and other ministers as "fellow workers with God" (v. 1), but he makes plain that his role in this shared work is a subordinate function: an ambassador. Remember that an ambassador does not set policy or principle but delivers the judgments and determinations of the ultimate sovereign.

Elsewhere Paul identifies the various offices of the church as gifts of the exalted Son. He writes to the Ephesians of the gifts given by the Son upon his ascension to the Father's throne (Eph. 4:7–10). "And he gave the apostles, the prophets, the evangelists, the shepherds and teachers, to equip the saints for the work of ministry, for building up the body of Christ" (vv. 11–12). Paul views the offices of the church as a gift of God. Further, he believes they serve to prepare the "saints for the work of ministry" and, thus, they equip every member of the body "for building up the body of Christ." But the offices do so by ministering the Word. Notice that each of the five offices described here are unique, but they all share a common, determinative trait: they are characterized by stewardship of the Word of God.[34]

Apostles are sent to proclaim the Word.

Prophets are given insight into the Word.

Evangelists are commissioned to preach the Word.

Shepherds are called to guide, protect, and feed with the Word.

Teachers are authorized to instruct in the Word.

The offices of the church are gifts of God, and their very nature points to the fact that their ongoing exercise must be sustained by God's continued speech in and through his Word. Their very nature is ministerial. They are ec-centric, dependent upon the leadership and life provided from outside (Gk. *ek*, meaning "out of").

34. John Calvin, *The Epistles of Paul the Apostle to the Galatians, Ephesians, Philippians, and Colossians*, Calvin's Commentaries, ed. David W. Torrance and Thomas F. Torrance, trans. T. H. L. Parker (Grand Rapids: Eerdmans, 1965), 178 (on Eph. 4:11).

Yet we need to remember that ministerial authority is genuine authority. That these offices and ministries are dependent upon triune grace does not mean they are haphazard or arbitrary places wherein God might show up. No, Paul spoke to the church in Colossae: "Let the word of Christ dwell in you richly" (Col. 3:16). The Word really dwells in them. The Word does not merely come time and again from outside but actually indwells or tabernacles among them. There is a promised presence and a pledged preservation by the Word. When Jesus initially commissioned his followers to go minister in his name, he did say that they should "go therefore and make disciples of all nations, baptizing them in the name of the Father and of the Son and of the Holy Spirit, teaching them to observe all that I have commanded you" (Matt. 28:19–20). But he only gives this commission after declaring, "All authority in heaven and on earth has been given to me" (v. 18) and before promising, "Behold, I am with you always, to the end of the age" (v. 20). Jesus has ensured the success of the church's mission through the ages with his presence. This does not guarantee perfection in its path, but it does point to his presence throughout and his promised glory at the end.[35]

In each of these ways, the catholic shape of ecclesial authority is honored, though it is reformed by noting its location in the economy of triune grace and, therefore, by remembering that its effectiveness is always dependent upon God's action. Reformational ecclesiology testifies about the church in all her catholic fullness, but it does so cognizant of the tendency to view her apart from Christ and his Spirit. These three habits of thought that permeate Reformational ecclesiology help point us back to the theocentric and gracious context of ecclesial authority. In this way three theological moves are being made, inasmuch as there is a genuine affirmation (1) of churchly authority and appreciation of its concrete reality, (2) of the vital connection of the churchly authority with Christ's agency, and (3) of the subordinate

---

35. Philip Schaff notes that the error of "popery," that is, the Roman Catholic faith and practice regarding ecclesial authority and the role of the papacy, is impatience. Schaff argues that infallibility in the church is not wrong per se, but it is identified as present now in the church by Roman Catholics, when the New Testament and the catholic tradition have looked toward its eschatological fulfillment in glory (*Principle of Protestantism*, 179n).

character of churchly authority, dependent upon and judged by the divine provision. In all three forms, the church's role is affirmed as a genuine social entity and a concrete community. Yet each form also locates the church as subservient to the primary agency of the Triune God. In so doing, they help contextualize the catholic shape of *sola Scriptura* by locating Scripture's final authority within the nexus of churchly practices and offices instituted and sustained by the very same Triune God who inspired those Holy Scriptures.

4

A Ruled Reading Reformed

The Role of the Church's Confession in Biblical Interpretation

The rule of faith (*regula fidei*) plays a central role in recent attempts to retrieve theological interpretation of Scripture, as indeed it must in any mode of hermeneutical inquiry that would reconnect with patristic, medieval, and Reformational habits of interpretation in the wake of modernity.[1] The most compelling attempts to retrieve the *regula fidei* for biblical interpretation to date are those characterized less by reliance upon the resources of philosophical and cultural

---

This chapter was originally published in a slightly different form as "A Ruled Reading Reformed: The Role of the Church's Confession in Biblical Interpretation," *International Journal of Systematic Theology* 14, no. 2 (April 2012): 177–93. Used by permission.

1. For an introduction to this discussion, see Kathryn Greene-McCreight, "Rule of Faith," in Kevin J. Vanhoozer, ed., *Dictionary for Theological Interpretation of the Bible* (Grand Rapids: Baker, 2005), 703–4; Daniel J. Treier, *Introducing Theological Interpretation of Scripture: Recovering a Christian Practice* (Grand Rapids: Baker, 2008), chap. 2; Stephen E. Fowl, *Theological Interpretation of Scripture* (Eugene, OR: Cascade, 2009), 24–31.

anthropology and more by confidence in traditional resources of dogmatic theology and ecclesiology.[2] While general theories of communal
rationality are not without merit when it comes to theological reflection
on this topic—one thinks here especially of Alasdair MacIntyre's notion of "tradition-based rationality"—general theories are in and of
themselves insufficient for the task. Given the church's unique status
as the people of God, the body of Christ, and the temple of the Holy
Spirit, the most operative concepts for thinking about the relation
between the church's confession and biblical exegesis are those drawn
from the trinitarian "economy of salvation and the pattern of divine
authority" exhibited therein.[3] Working from this premise, the purpose
of the present chapter is to provide an argument for a "ruled reading" of
Holy Scripture on the basis of Reformed theological and ecclesiological
principles.[4] The argument is an exercise in Reformed *ressourcement*,
what we are calling "Reformed catholicity." That is to say, it is an
exercise in theological remembrance and retrieval, seeking to recover
the habits of theological thought and argumentation belonging to an
older confessional dogmatics, and to the broad churchly tradition of
biblical interpretation that lies both behind and beside it, for the sake
of contemporary theological renewal.[5]

The call for a ruled reading of the Bible is not novel, of course,
when considered from the perspective of church history or from the
perspective of recent hermeneutical literature.[6] A distinctly Reformed
approach to the topic is nevertheless worth pursuing in the pres-

2. Reinhard Hütter, *Suffering Divine Things: Theology as Church Practice* (Grand
Rapids: Eerdmans, 2000), 176–87; Kevin J. Vanhoozer, *The Drama of Doctrine: A
Canonical-Linguistic Approach to Christian Theology* (Louisville: Westminster John
Knox, 2005), chap. 6 and conclusion; Matthew J. Levering, *Participatory Biblical
Exegesis: A Theology of Biblical Interpretation* (Notre Dame: University of Notre
Dame Press, 2008), esp. chap. 5; and Robert W. Jenson, *Canon and Creed* (Louisville:
Westminster John Knox, 2010).

3. Vanhoozer, *Drama of Doctrine*, 164.

4. The present chapter expands upon an argument more briefly made in Scott R.
Swain, *Trinity, Revelation, and Reading: A Theological Introduction to the Bible and
Its Interpretation* (London: T&T Clark, 2011), chap. 4.

5. We are greatly indebted in this exercise to Richard A. Muller, *Post-Reformation
Reformed Dogmatics: The Rise and Development of Reformed Orthodoxy, ca. 1520
to ca. 1725*, 4 vols. (Grand Rapids: Baker, 2003), esp. vols. 1 and 2.

6. See also the relevant recent movements of theological retrieval described in our
introduction, several of which involve exegetical retrieval.

ent climate for a number of reasons. First, the broader culture of biblical interpretation (both critical and evangelical) still remains largely skeptical toward the prospect of creedal/confessional biblical interpretation.[7] In this context, expounding the theological rationale for such an approach is anything but redundant. Second, while much has been written by way of recovering patristic and medieval practices of biblical interpretation,[8] and by way of articulating a more or less Roman Catholic approach to theological interpretation,[9] it is still common to suppose that a specifically Protestant approach to interpretation is inconsistent with a ruled reading of the Bible, whether it is because the latter represents an illegitimate ecclesiastical constraint upon free and rational inquiry,[10] or because it allows later historical developments (i.e., the creed) to guide exegesis instead of the Bible's own literary-historical categories and contexts.[11] Recent work has

7. Jenson, *Canon and Creed*, 2. On the historical reasons for this, see Michael Legaspi, *The Death of Scripture and the Rise of Biblical Studies* (Oxford: Oxford University Press, 2010); and Jeffrey L. Morrow, "The Bible in Captivity: Hobbes, Spinoza, and the Politics of Defining Religion," *Pro Ecclesia* 19 (2010): 285–99.

8. John J. O'Keefe and R. R. Reno, *Sanctified Vision: An Introduction to Early Christian Interpretation of the Bible* (Baltimore: Johns Hopkins University Press, 2005); D. H. Williams, *Evangelicals and Tradition: The Formative Influence of the Early Church* (Grand Rapids: Baker, 2005); Jason Byassee, *Praise Seeking Understanding: Reading the Psalms with Augustine* (Grand Rapids: Eerdmans, 2007); Henri de Lubac, *Medieval Exegesis*, 3 vols., trans. Marc Sebanc and E. M. Macierowski (Grand Rapids: Eerdmans, 1998–2009); Thomas Weinandy, Daniel Keating, and John Yocum, eds., *Aquinas on Scripture: A Critical Introduction to His Commentaries* (London: T&T Clark, 2005).

9. Levering, *Participatory Biblical Exegesis*. Consider also Peter S. Williamson, *Catholic Principles for Interpreting Scripture: A Study of the Pontifical Biblical Commission's "The Interpretation of the Bible in the Church"* (Rome: Pontifical Biblical Institute, 2001); and Luke Timothy Johnson and William S. Kurz, *The Future of Catholic Biblical Scholarship: A Constructive Conversation* (Grand Rapids: Eerdmans, 2002). In terms of the relationship between the church and biblical interpretation, the proposals of Reinhard Hütter and Robert Jenson should perhaps be categorized here, as Hütter's notion of the church's enhypostaticization by the Spirit (*Suffering Divine Things*, 132–45) and Jenson's construal of the episcopate (*Systematic Theology* [New York: Oxford University Press, 1997], 1:39–41) appear from a Reformed ecclesiological perspective to be indicative of an ecclesiology *in excessu*. See our discussion of the christological, pneumatological, and ecclesiological context of theology in chap. 1.

10. John Barton, "Historical-critical Approaches," in John Barton, ed., *The Cambridge Companion to Biblical Interpretation* (Cambridge: Cambridge University Press, 1998), esp. 16–19.

11. This concern is echoed throughout D. A. Carson, "Systematic Theology and Biblical Theology," in Desmond Alexander and Brian Rosner, eds., *New Dictionary*

contributed a great deal to challenging this common supposition by demonstrating the need to situate certain Protestant convictions about the Bible, church tradition, and interpretive reason within the more expansive and fundamental context of the Trinity and the unfolding economy of salvation.[12] We hope to build upon these contributions by suggesting a Reformed account of the way in which the rule of faith may be seen as a legitimate extension of the church's teaching authority and therefore as an aid to realizing the ends of that teaching authority in relation to Scripture.[13]

A third reason to pursue a Reformed approach to a ruled reading of the Bible is that Reformed and Presbyterian churches, at least in the United States, continue to struggle with what it means to relate the canon of Holy Scripture to the confession of the church. This struggle is visible not only in debates about confessional subscription,[14] but in recent debates about how the church should deal with biblical exegesis that appears to contradict the church's confessional documents.[15] Achieving clarity on such matters requires a coherent theological framework for thinking about the relationship between ecclesial creed and scriptural canon.

Fourth, while individuals may undertake the work of dogmatics, dogmatics is not the work of the private individual but is rather the work of the church. The individual who engages in dogmatics does so therefore in a self-consciously ecclesial persona, as a person speaking

---

of Biblical Theology (Downers Grove, IL: InterVarsity, 2000), 89–104. We address these objections in chap. 5 below.

12. Vanhoozer, *Drama of Doctrine*; and John Webster, "Biblical Reasoning," *Anglican Theological Review* 90 (2008): 733–51.

13. In a recent discussion of episcopacy, Jenson acknowledges that "there may be other ways in which a church may have a functioning magisterium" apart from the episcopate (*Canon and Creed*, 71). The present chapter seeks to articulate one of these unnamed "other ways" and to explore how such an alternative might warrant and guide our use of the *regula fidei* in biblical interpretation. This chapter offers specific ecclesiastical implications of the ecclesiology offered above in chap. 1, extending further its analysis of the economy of grace within which churchly theological work is to be done into matters regarding the specific accredited and authoritative exercise of that ecclesiological action.

14. See, for example, the essays in David W. Hall, ed., *The Practice of Confessional Subscription* (Lanham, MD: University Press of America, 1995).

15. Recent North American ecclesiastical debates pertaining to the doctrine of justification are a case in point.

in and on behalf of the church's public confession. The relevance of our topic follows from this fact. If exegesis is the lifeblood of dogmatics, then a truly churchly dogmatics can only flourish on the basis of a churchly exegesis. Establishing a coherent account of churchly exegesis requires accounting for the role of the rule of faith within that exegesis. For all of the above reasons, we may conclude with A. T. B. McGowan that "the need to define properly the relationship between Scripture and our confessional statements is both vital and urgent."[16]

With an eye to our topic's need and relevance, therefore, we turn to the matter at hand: What is the role of the church's confession in biblical interpretation? Delineating an answer to this question will require two steps: We will first consider what it means to speak of the church as an authorized reading community according to the Reformed confession. Building on this discussion, we will then consider the relationship between the rule of faith and biblical interpretation. As we will see, the rule of faith is an ecclesiastically authorized representation of scriptural teaching whose hermeneutical function is to provide not only a starting point for biblical exegesis but also to direct exegesis to its goal, which is the exposition of each particular text of Holy Scripture within the overarching context and purpose of the whole counsel of God.

The Church as an Authorized Reading Community

For Christians, reading is an inherently communal enterprise. And reading is a communal enterprise for the same reasons that Christianity is a communal enterprise. God's purpose in the covenant of grace is not simply to reconcile individual persons to himself. When God reconciles individual persons to himself in the covenant of grace, he also binds those persons to other persons, creating a new humanity and an interdependent body (Eph. 2:11–20; 1 Cor. 12:12).[17] In God's design, this body's growth in the knowledge of God

16. McGowan, *The Divine Authenticity of Scripture: Retrieving an Evangelical Heritage* (Downers Grove, IL: IVP Academic, 2007), 187.

17. Stephen R. Holmes, *Listening to the Past: The Place of Tradition in Theology* (Grand Rapids: Baker Academic, 2002), 22–26. Again, see our discussion of ecclesiology and the habits of theology above in chap. 1.

is not caused by God alone (Col. 2:19). Rather, the Lord nourishes his body and causes it to grow by means of the body's own proper agency and work.[18] The church "builds itself up" (Eph. 4:16). The knowledge of the gospel's God is a knowledge obtained and sustained "with all the saints" (Eph. 3:18; cf. 2 Tim. 3:14–15). For this reason, the Christian reader of Holy Scripture finds her place as a reader among the company of those who have been brought from death to life by the Word of God, gathered together in a common fellowship under the Lord's guidance and teaching, and equipped by the Lord to instruct and edify one another in the shared faith. The Christian reader "is no isolated worker, but . . . is in his way the organ of restored humanity."[19] Christian reading is thus a communal enterprise.

As a reader in community, the Christian reader of Holy Scripture stands in a particular relation to the authority of that community. The Lord who liberates sinners from a state of alienation and disorder binds them to himself and to one another in a community that is authorized to serve Holy Scripture in various concrete ways. It is important of course to emphasize that this community in no way authorizes or establishes Holy Scripture. The church is a "creature of the Word,"[20] established upon the testimony of the apostles and prophets (Eph. 2:20). Nevertheless, to say that Holy Scripture is the supreme and self-authenticating authority for the faith and life of God's people is not to say that it is the sole authority for the faith and life of God's people. *Sola Scriptura* ("Scripture alone") must be distinguished from *solo Scriptura* ("Scripture only") when it comes to interpreting and understanding the Bible.

18. See also our discussion of these issues above in chap. 3, in the section "Guarding the Good Deposit: Dogmatic Tools for Thinking Scripture and Tradition Together." For a more detailed account in which we are in much agreement, see John Webster, "Evangelical Ecclesiology," *Ecclesiology* 1 (2004): 9–35.

19. Abraham Kuyper, *Principles of Sacred Theology*, trans. J. Hendrik De Vries (Grand Rapids: Eerdmans, 1968), 581.

20. Christoph Schwöbel, "The Creature of the Word: Recovering the Ecclesiology of the Reformers," in Colin Gunton and Daniel Hardy, eds., *On Being the Church: Essays on the Christian Community* (Edinburgh: T&T Clark, 1989), 110–55. See our discussion of this theme above in the section "Guarding the Good Deposit: Dogmatic Tools for Thinking Scripture and Tradition Together" in chap. 3.

Though Reformed Protestants have diligently defended the supreme authority of Scripture over the church, they have—at least historically—also articulated an understanding of the church's subordinate or ministerial authority for serving Scripture. The church is an ordered and orderly organism, divinely authorized to serve Holy Scripture in various ways. Sixteenth-century Protestant divine William Whitaker provides a representative summary of four ways in which Christ has authorized the church to serve his sacred Word.[21] According to Whitaker:

1. "First, the church is the witness and guardian of the sacred writings, and discharges, in this respect, as it were the function of a notary." God has delivered his Holy Scriptures to his people and authorized her to keep them (cf. Deut. 31:9; Rom. 3:2). Nevertheless, Whitaker insists, the authority of Scripture is not established by its guardians "but on account of" Scripture's "own trustworthiness."

2. "The second office of the church is, to distinguish and discern the true, sincere, and genuine scriptures from the spurious, false, and supposititious" (cf. 1 Cor. 14:37; 2 Thess. 2:1–2).[22] According to Whitaker, "for the performance of this function," the church "hath the Spirit of Christ to enable it to distinguish the true from the false: it knows the voice of its spouse; it is endued with the highest prudence, and is able to try the spirits" (cf. 1 Thess. 5:20–21; 1 John 4:1).

3. "The third office of the church is to publish, set forth, preach, and promulgate the scriptures; wherein it discharges the function of a herald, who ought to pronounce with a loud voice the decrees and edicts of the king, to omit nothing, and to add nothing of his own" (cf. Isa. 40:9; Rom. 10:16; 2 Cor. 5:19).

21. For what follows, see William Whitaker, *A Disputation on Holy Scripture*, trans. William Fitzgerald (1588; repr., Morgan, PA: Soli Deo Gloria, 2000), 283–84. Cf. Francis Turretin, *Institutes of Elenctic Theology*, trans. George Musgrave Giger (Phillipsburg, NJ: Presbyterian & Reformed, 1992), 1:90.

22. On the oft-neglected communal dimension of this activity, see Roger Nicole, "The Canon of the New Testament," in *Standing Forth: Collected Writings of Roger Nicole* (Fearn, Ross-shire, UK: Christian Focus, 2002), esp. 97–101.

4. "The fourth office of the church is to expound and interpret the scriptures; wherein its function is that of an interpreter. Here it should introduce no fictions of its own, but explain the scriptures by the scriptures" (cf. Matt. 13:52; Rom. 12:6; 1 Cor. 14:3, 29; Eph. 4:11; 2 Tim. 2:15).

By way of summary, then, the church is that community created and authorized by the Word of God in order that it might obediently guard, discern, proclaim, and interpret the Word of God.

These four mandates are fulfilled in a rich variety of ways in the life of the church. Parents instruct children in the sacred writings from their youth (Deut. 6:7; Eph. 6:4; 2 Tim. 3:15). Neighbor edifies neighbor by "speaking the truth in love" (Eph. 4:15; cf. 1 Thess. 4:18; 5:11; Heb. 10:25). The Scriptures are read aloud, prayed, proclaimed, and sung in public worship week after week (Col. 3:16; 1 Tim. 4:13). Alongside and in service of these avenues for receiving and spreading the Word of God, the Spirit also sets apart certain persons within the church to serve as publicly authorized ministers of biblical teaching (Eph. 4:11; 1 Pet. 4:10–11; 1 Tim. 5:20; 2 Tim. 4:2; Titus 2:15; cf. James 3:1). The same Spirit who laid the foundation for the church's knowledge of God through his work of inspiring the prophetic and apostolic Scriptures builds upon that foundation through his work of calling, instructing, and commissioning the church's "accredited leaders" (Eph. 2:20; 4:11–12; 1 Cor. 3:10–15; 12:28).[23] Such leaders are, among other things, commissioned to proclaim "the whole counsel of God" (Acts 20:27; cf. 20:32), their commission being accompanied by the Spirit's gifts of teaching and discernment (Rom. 12:6–7; 1 Cor. 14:3, 29; 1 Thess. 5:21).

In accordance with the variety of ways in which the church exercises its authority in relation to God's Word, the Reformed divide the church's *potestas interpretandi*, or "power of interpretation," into two spheres.[24] On the one hand, the *potestas privata*, or "the

---

23. N. T. Wright, *Scripture and the Authority of God* (London: SPCK, 2005), 100–104. Note the order in 1 Cor. 12:28: "God has appointed in the church first apostles, second prophets, third teachers."

24. For fuller discussion of the relationship between the public teaching office and the private right of believers to interpret the Bible, see *Synopsis purioris theologiae,*

power of private judgment," concerns the right and privilege that all believers enjoy "to interpret Scripture for personal edification and the building-up of faith." On the other hand, the *potestas publica,* or "the power of public interpretation," does not belong to "all Christians but accompanies a special calling to public ministry" and "is supported by special gifts."[25] James Bannerman explains the purpose of this second power of interpretation:

> Instead of perpetuating or renewing in every successive age the miracle of Pentecost, there has been instituted a perpetual and standing ordinance of interpreters and teachers, who may both translate and explain the original Scriptures for the benefit of the members of the Church at large. . . . They are in a peculiar manner the ambassadors of Christ on behalf of men, commissioned to preach His Gospel in His name; and speaking with authority, not their own, but His, to unfold and expound and proclaim the message of His mercy to his people.[26]

The power of public interpretation is a ministerial authority. On the one hand, it is a true authority: Jesus commanded the Jews of his day to acknowledge the authority of the scribes and the Pharisees (Matt. 23:1–3). Likewise, the author of Hebrews instructs his readers to submit to their leaders (Heb. 13:17). Accordingly, Bannerman states: "When the Church through its appointed organs declares the truth, it is to be heard not only because it is truth, and because it is in accordance with the Word of God as revealed in the Bible, but also because the Church is an ordinance of God appointed to declare it."[27] On the other hand, because such authority is a ministerial authority, it is accountable to God's Word in Holy Scripture: and so Jesus also rebuked the scribes and Pharisees for undermining God's Word

6th ed., ed. Herman Bavinck (Leiden: Didericum Donner, 1881), 5.27–39; with Muller, *Post-Reformation Reformed Dogmatics*, 2:468–69.

25. Richard A. Muller, "potestas interpretandi sive iudicandi," in *Dictionary of Latin and Greek Theological Terms: Drawn Principally from Protestant Scholastic Theology* (Grand Rapids: Baker, 1985), 233.

26. James Bannerman, *The Church of Christ: A Treatise on the Nature, Powers, Ordinances, Discipline and Government of the Christian Church* (1869; repr., New York: Westminster, 2002), 1:279–80.

27. Ibid., 1:282.

by teaching things that did not comport with it but rather hindered others from heeding its commands (Matt. 15:1–9). Similarly, Paul pronounced a curse on anyone—including apostle or angel!—who would teach another Christ or another gospel than that which had been revealed by God to and through him (Gal. 1:8–9).

The pattern of ecclesial authority exhibited in the Gospel of Matthew further illumines the matter at hand. According to Matthew, the source of the church's authority lies in the exalted Son of Man who, having completed the earthly mission given to him by the Father (cf. 21:33–42), has received "all authority in heaven and on earth" (28:18). The Son of Man's authority is in a very important sense unique and incommunicable. He is teacher and instructor; his disciples are brothers and pupils (23:8–10). However, the fact that the Lord alone possesses all authority in the church does not mean that he is the only authority in the church. As Matthew 28:18–20 demonstrates, the exalted Lord exercises his unique authority *by authorizing* the church to make disciples. Being set *under* the Lord's supreme authority puts the church *in* authority to fulfill his commission (cf. 8:9).[28] The church's authority to make disciples includes the activities of baptismal initiation into God's triune fellowship and catechetical instruction in the Lord's teaching. Concerning the latter point, it is relevant to note that the apostles are commissioned to teach "*all*" that Jesus has commanded them, which certainly echoes the Old Testament prophets' commission to speak all that the Lord commanded them (Deut. 18:18; Jer. 1:7, 17), nothing more and nothing less (cf. Deut. 4:2; Rev. 22:18–19). To his command to make disciples, the exalted Jesus adds the promise of his presence (Matt. 28:20), which in Matthew's Gospel is the seal of Jesus's authority upon ecclesial activity (18:18–20). The exalted Son of Man thus exercises his authority—"on earth as it is in heaven" (6:10)—*through* the agency of the church, the community authorized to serve his lordly commission and accompanied by his lordly presence.

A survey of Matthew's teaching on ecclesial authority must include mention of Matthew 16:18–19. Though space forbids engaging the

28. Cf. Oliver O'Donovan, *The Desire of the Nations: Rediscovering the Roots of Political Theology* (Cambridge: Cambridge University Press, 1996), 90.

nettle of exegetical and historical issues associated with this passage,[29] a couple of points can be made. First, as in the case of 28:18–20, we see that the Lord's authority to build the church, of which he is the foundational "cornerstone" (see 21:42; cf. 1 Pet. 2:7), is exercised through the agency of Peter and the apostles, who also belong to the foundation of the ecclesial edifice (16:18; cf. Eph. 2:20). Second, it is through the apostles' teaching authority (this is the likely significance of "the keys of the kingdom" in 16:19; cf. Luke 11:52[30]) that heaven's authority will be exercised on earth and that the church will prevail even in the face of death (16:18–19).

One further point is relevant to the present discussion. According to Matthew's portrait, it is not only the apostles who will exercise teaching authority in Christ's church. Matthew also envisions the ministry of scribes "trained for the kingdom of heaven" (13:52). It does not seem that the First Evangelist wishes to limit this group to the twelve—he speaks of "*every* scribe trained for the kingdom of heaven." Rather, the point seems to be that, just as God's Word through Moses was authoritatively perpetuated through the ministry of scribes who sat in "Moses' seat" (23:2–3), so too God's Word through the apostles will be authoritatively perpetuated through the ministry of scribes trained for the kingdom of heaven, who will bring out of their "treasure what is new and what is old" (13:52; cf. 5:19 on "what is old"; and 13:11, 35 on "what is new"). While there is analogy between the prophetic-apostolic teaching authority and that of their respective scribes, there is also disanalogy. The teaching ministry of the apostles and prophets belongs to the foundation of the church (16:18). The teaching ministry of the scribes can only build upon that foundation, which is its measure or "canon." If the scribal tradition fails to perpetuate everything taught by the Lord through his prophets and apostles (and only those things), then it will make void the Word of God (15:1–9) and invite divine woes upon itself (23:13–36; cf. Mark 12:38). However, if the scribal tradition is faithful to perpetuate

29. For a recent overview of the history of interpretation, see Ulrich Luz, *Studies in Matthew*, trans. Rosemary Selle (Grand Rapids: Eerdmans, 2005), chap. 9.

30. W. D. Davies and Dale C. Allison, Jr., *A Critical and Exegetical Commentary on the Gospel According to Saint Matthew*, International Critical Commentary (Edinburgh: T&T Clark, 1991), 2:634–41.

everything taught by the Lord through his prophets and apostles (and only those things), then it may expect the Lord's blessing upon its divinely authorized service.

For these reasons, the church's accredited teachers faithfully fulfill their ministries when they demonstrate that their teaching is nothing other than the teaching of the Holy Spirit speaking in Holy Scripture.[31] As Dietrich Bonhoeffer states, "Genuine authority knows that it can only exist in the service of the One who alone has authority. Genuine authority knows that it is bound in the strictest sense by the words of Jesus, 'You have one teacher, and you are all brothers'" (Matt. 23:8).[32] The teacher in Christ's church thus exhibits a brotherly exercise of authority when he shows "the reasons and bases of his interpretation so clearly and certainly that also others who themselves do not have the gift of interpretation may be able to understand and grasp them."[33] In other words, because they serve Christ's sovereign self-revelation in his prophetic-apostolic Word, teachers may never simply say, "Because we said so," to authorize their teaching. Instead they must always *say* and *show*, "Thus says the Lord." In doing so, the church's teachers may hope to gain the Spirit-enabled "Amen" of the hearing church (thus Chemnitz).

To be sure, demonstrating "the reasons and bases" of interpretation is not a matter of facile proof texting. Nor does the work of demonstration demand that the church only speak in a biblical idiom. The reformers learned very quickly that the latter restriction would only undermine rather than serve the ministry of the Word.[34] The church is free to use a conceptual idiom different from that of Holy Scripture—indeed, within Scripture itself we find a different idiom in John than we find in Paul. However, the church is responsible for

31. Westminster Confession of Faith, chap. 1.10, in Philip Schaff, *The Creeds of Christendom: With a History and Critical Notes*, 6th ed. (1931; repr., Grand Rapids: Baker, 1996), 3:598–673.
32. Dietrich Bonhoeffer, *Life Together and Prayerbook of the Bible*, Dietrich Bonhoeffer Works 5 (Minneapolis: Fortress, 2005), 107.
33. Martin Chemnitz, *Examination of the Council of Trent*, vol. 1, trans. Fred Kramer (St. Louis: Concordia, 1971), 216.
34. John Calvin, *Institutes of the Christian Religion*, ed. John McNeill, trans. Ford Lewis Battles (Philadelphia: Westminster, 1960), 1:123–24 (1.13.3). See Muller, *Post-Reformation Reformed Dogmatics*, 4:59–74. See our lengthy discussion of this complex issue in chap. 5.

demonstrating the transparency of its idiom to the teaching of the sacred writings. It is responsible for demonstrating that its teaching is truly a re-presentation of biblical doctrine.

It is important to acknowledge the presence of the church's teaching authority when it comes to biblical interpretation, because God has appointed this authority as an aid to reading Holy Scripture. Just as the Spirit sent Philip to help the Ethiopian eunuch read Isaiah (Acts 8:30–35), and just as Paul charged Timothy to teach those who would be able to teach others also (2 Tim. 2:2), similarly God has provided his church not only with a supreme standard for faith and life *in* Holy Scripture, he has also *through* Holy Scripture generated an authorized sphere of ecclesial reality that is charged to assist us in reading the Scriptures.[35] The church's teaching authority does not exist in order to exclude others from interpreting and understanding God's Word. Rather, the church's teaching authority exists in order to communicate (i.e., "make common") the treasures of God's Word to all of God's people so that they too might have full communion (i.e., "share as equals") in those treasures (cf. Matt. 13:52). For this reason, biblical interpretation flourishes when it operates within and according to the authorized sphere of ecclesial reality created and governed by the Spirit of God through the Word of God.

Historically, the church has acknowledged two servants as particularly trustworthy aids when it comes to interpreting the Bible: "the rule of faith" and "the rule of love."[36] The rule of faith and the rule of love provide normative summaries of the Bible's doctrinal and ethical teaching. They are not teachers per se, but instead function as instruments of the church's teaching authority.[37] As such, they serve as important aids in biblical interpretation. These rules are found in various expressions throughout the life of the church, from the in-

35. Francis Watson deploys Hans-Georg Gadamer's concept of a text's *Wirkungsgeschichte* to great effect in describing the ways in which the Holy Scripture "generates" a community that understands and confesses the Word of God. See his "Hermeneutics and the Doctrine of Scripture: Why They Need Each Other," *International Journal of Systematic Theology* 12 (2010): 118–43, esp. 135–37.

36. See, for example, "The Second Helvetic Confession," in Philip Schaff, *The Creeds of Christendom: With a History and Critical Notes*, 6th ed. (1931; repr., Grand Rapids: Baker, 1996), 3:831–909 (chap. 2).

37. Cf. Westminster Confession of Faith, chap. 31, "Of Synods and Councils."

formal proclamation of evangelists to the more formal statements of ecclesiastical synods and assemblies. The latter forms possess greater authority than those expressed in the teaching of individual ministers, for they are usually products of a collective body of ministers, drawn in humble deference to the church's historic creeds and confessions, and endorsed by deliberating bodies of the church as a whole.[38] The remainder of the present essay will focus on the rule of faith in particular and upon its relationship to biblical interpretation.

The Rule of Faith and Biblical Interpretation

In his first epistle to Timothy, the apostle Paul charged his young protégé to avoid "myths and endless genealogies" and instead to pursue an exposition of the sacred writings that accords with "the economy of God that is by faith" (1 Tim. 1:4, trans. mine; cf. 4:6–16). There is, according to Paul, a kind of biblical interpretation that is absorbed with mythology and that promotes speculation, and there is a kind of biblical interpretation that accords with God's overarching economy of salvation and that promotes faith. It is the latter type of interpretation, as opposed to the former, that the rule of faith aids us in pursuing.

In the broadest sense, "the rule of faith" refers to any shorthand summary of "the faith that was once for all delivered to the saints" (Jude 3).[39] We see examples of such summaries within Holy Scripture itself. Deuteronomy 6:4–5, the *Shema*, summarizes the more extended presentation of the divine name revealed in the Pentateuch to that point: "Hear, O Israel: The LORD our God, the LORD is one." It also summarizes God's law, which is expounded at length in previous chapters of the Pentateuch: "You shall love the LORD your God with all your heart and with all your soul and with all your might." Similar confessional summaries appear in the New Testament as well. First Corinthians 8:6 is a christological elaboration of the *Shema*: "For us there is one God, the Father, from whom are all things and for whom we exist, and one Lord, Jesus Christ, through whom are all things

38. Kuyper, *Principles of Sacred Theology*, 576; also 591.
39. John Behr, *The Way to Nicaea*, The Formation of Christian Theology 1 (Crestwood, NY: St. Vladimir's Seminary Press, 2001), chap. 1; and Greene-McCreight, "Rule of Faith," 703–4.

and through whom we exist."[40] In Ephesians 4:4–6, Paul grounds his call to Christian unity in a trinitarian confession related to God's identity and his saving work in the church: "There is one body and one Spirit—just as you were called to the one hope that belongs to your call—one Lord, one faith, one baptism, one God and Father of all, who is over all and through all and in all." The expansion of these and other biblical summaries (e.g., 1 Cor. 12:4–6; 15:3–4; 1 Tim. 3:16) beyond the time of the New Testament therefore represents the faithful extension of an inner-biblical impulse. Indeed, confessional summarization—whether in praise, proclamation, or official confessional promulgation—is one of the most inherently appropriate responses to biblical revelation: "I will recount all of your wonderful deeds" (Ps. 9:1).[41] The biblical canon, we might say, naturally gives birth to ecclesial confession.[42] The rule of faith is a natural sign of Holy Scripture's regency.[43]

The use of trinitarian creedal summaries beyond the New Testament era likely originated with the need to provide baptismal candidates with a fixed form for confessing their faith in obedience to the Lord's command to baptize "in the name of the Father and of the Son and of the Holy Spirit" (Matt. 28:19).[44] "Two elements" that "remain constant" in these early summaries of the faith are (1) the triune name of "Father, Son, and Holy Spirit"; and (2) the gospel narrative of "the life, death, and resurrection of Jesus Christ."[45] Such summaries have since come to fulfill various functions within the church, including their function as subordinate standards to which the church's office-bearers subscribe and in accordance with which they pledge to teach in fulfillment of their calling.

---

40. Richard Bauckham, *Jesus and the God of Israel: God Crucified and Other Studies on the New Testament's Christology of Divine Identity* (Grand Rapids: Eerdmans, 2008), 26–30.

41. See our comments on similar statements in Psalm 145 regarding the churchly recounting of God's deeds in chap. 3.

42. Frances Young, *The Making of the Creeds* (London: SCM, 2002), 12–13.

43. Cf. Kuyper, *Principles of Sacred Theology*, 570.

44. Young, *Making of the Creeds*, 6.

45. Jaroslav Pelikan, *The Christian Tradition: A History of the Development of Doctrine*, vol. 1, *The Emergence of the Catholic Tradition (100–600)* (Chicago: University of Chicago Press, 1971), 117.

One of the earliest and certainly most enduring examples of the rule of faith is the Apostles' Creed. Though not stated in so many words in Scripture, the Apostles' Creed is nevertheless a faithful *re*-presentation of scriptural teaching. The creed faithfully represents scriptural teaching in at least two senses. First, it summarizes the plain teaching of Holy Scripture. As Augustine observed long ago, the rule of faith is drawn from the clearer passages of Scripture, not from its more obscure passages.[46] Second, the creed is a faithful representation of scriptural teaching because it summarizes that teaching in a way that reflects Scripture's own proportions and purpose. The rule of faith sets Scripture's most recurring themes or "common places" in their proper relations to one another and in relation to Scripture's overarching purpose.

To speak of "proportion" suggests that biblical interpretation has an aesthetic dimension and that the rule of faith serves in training our senses to perceive Scripture's fullness, order, and beauty.[47] According to Irenaeus's famous analogy, the rule of faith functions like the pattern for a mosaic, helping us see how all the various tiles fit together to form the picture of a handsome king.[48] Thus, for example, the Apostles' Creed presents the splendor of biblical truth in biblical proportions by confessing (1) Scripture's main subject matter, the Holy Trinity, "from whom and through whom and to whom are all things" (Rom. 11:36); (2) the overarching shape of the divine economy in creation, redemption, and consummation; and (3) at least by implication, a host of other essential doctrinal themes, including the following: the goodness of creation (God made it; God assumed it in the incarnation—"our Lord . . . was conceived by the Holy Ghost"; God will raise it—"I believe in . . . the resurrection of the body"); the centrality of the evangelical events in redemptive history; as well

46. See Augustine, *On Christian Doctrine, Nicene and Post-Nicene Fathers* (Grand Rapids: Eerdmans, 1993), 2:539 (2.9.14). According to William Perkins, the rule of faith "is a summary of the Scriptures, drawn from its well-known and clear parts" (*The Art of Prophesying* [1606; repr., Edinburgh: Banner of Truth, 1996], 26–27). See also Whitaker, *Disputation*, 472, 474, 484.

47. Jens Zimmermann, *Recovering Theological Hermeneutics: An Incarnational-Trinitarian Theory of Interpretation* (Grand Rapids: Baker, 2004), 307–16.

48. Irenaeus, *Against Heresies*, Ante-Nicene Fathers 1 (Grand Rapids: Eerdmans, 1996), 326 (1.8.1).

as doctrines such as the church, the forgiveness of sins, and the life everlasting. Moreover, by orienting its confessors to Scripture's main subject matter, the Triune God, and to the scriptural record of his wonderful works, the rule of faith also orients them to the supreme goal or purpose of Scripture, "which is to give all glory to God."[49] To use Irenaeus's analogy, the rule of faith helps us appreciate the central role of the messianic king in the divine economy and thereby helps us perceive his preeminent status as the radiance of God (cf. Heb. 1:3). The rule of faith aids doxological reading.[50]

The rule of faith thus equips us to read the various parts of Scripture in light of the whole and with an eye to Scripture's ultimate purpose—both good strategies for reading any book. Here we may invoke Calvin's famous image: as spectacles help the reader follow the letters on a page, so the rule of faith helps us follow "the *pattern of sound teaching*" (2 Tim. 1:13 NIV) contained in Holy Scripture.

As is the case with the church's teaching authority in general, the rule of faith always stands in a relation of dependence upon the scriptural source and fountain of truth. For this reason, its authoritative status may never be reckoned as "self-evident" but must always be established by way of interpretive "demonstration and argument."[51] Each generation is charged with the task not only of defending the faith once delivered to the saints but also with the task of demonstrating the biblical foundations of that faith through biblical exegesis (cf. Acts 17:11). When this exegetical task is ignored or forsaken, theology quickly degenerates into an arid repetition of dogmatic symbols. Furthermore, because the church can and has erred in its confession,[52] its

49. Westminster Confession of Faith, chap. 1.5. See also Second Helvetic Confession, chap. 2; and Barth's brief but helpful discussion of this scriptural impulse, following Amandus Polanus, in *Church Dogmatics*, vol. 1, *The Doctrine of the Word of God*, part 2, ed. G. W. Bromiley and T. F. Torrance, trans. G. T. Thomson and Harold Knight (Edinburgh: T&T Clark, 1956), 721–22.

50. For further reflections on the role of the Apostles' Creed in biblical interpretation, see Jenson, *Canon and Creed*, chap. 5.

51. Oliver O'Donovan, *Church in Crisis: The Gay Crisis and the Anglican Communion* (Eugene, OR: Wipf & Stock, 2008), 79.

52. According to Anthony N. S. Lane, "*Sola Scriptura* is the statement that the church can err" ("*Sola Scriptura*? Making Sense of a Post-Reformation Slogan," in Philip E. Satterthwaite and David F. Wright, eds., *A Pathway into the Holy Scripture* [Grand Rapids: Eerdmans, 1994], 324).

various expressions of the rule of faith are always subject to revision and reform in light of the clear teaching of Holy Scripture, which remains "the supreme judge by which all controversies of religion are to be determined, and all decrees of councils, opinions of ancient writers, doctrines of men, and private spirits, are to be examined."[53]

Scripture is the supreme source of revealed teaching. The rule of faith is only a channel through which that revealed teaching flows.[54] However, this does not mean that the rule of faith is open to endless revision, as many modern understandings of *sola Scriptura*—and of *semper reformanda*—have supposed. "Christianity is one and not many and is not capable of continuous radical reinterpretation."[55] God has spoken in Holy Scripture; and the church by God's grace has made a faithful confession. In this regard, "dogmas"—the church's public and binding summaries of scriptural truth[56]—stand as "irreversible" expressions of the rule of faith, expressions with which all later summaries of the rule of faith must cohere and which all further summaries of the rule of faith must exhibit.[57] Church dogma, we might say, is a sign of Christ's victory, accomplished through Word and Spirit, within the common mind of the church. It is for this reason an ancient landmark that should not be moved.

Acts 15 recounts the paradigmatic instance of conciliar dogma.[58] Three features of this account are of particular relevance to the present discussion. First, it is "the apostles and elders" who assemble to consider the matter (15:6). Though it is unremarkable that the apostles would be involved in resolving the issue under dispute, given their role in leading the Jerusalem Church since its inception (2:42–43; 4:33, 35, 37; 5:29; 6:1–6; 8:1, 14; 9:27; 11:1), it is somewhat surprising that the elders should have such a significant role to play, considering the fact that they have been mentioned for the first time only in 11:30. What is the relevance of the elders' inclusion in Luke's narrative at this point? It seems Luke wishes to show that a transition in leadership is taking

53. Westminster Confession of Faith, chap. 1.10.
54. Bavinck, *Reformed Dogmatics* (Grand Rapids: Baker, 2003), 1:493.
55. Bernard Ramm, *The Evangelical Heritage: A Study in Historical Theology* (1973; repr., Grand Rapids: Baker Books, 2000), 140.
56. For this understanding of dogma, see Bavinck, *Reformed Dogmatics*, 1:28–34.
57. Jenson, *Systematic Theology*, 1:36.
58. For fuller analysis of Acts 15, see chap. 3.

place.[59] As the apostles' foundational role in establishing the church is coming to an end (consider how Peter disappears from the narrative after Acts 15), the leadership of the early church is in the process of transitioning into the hands of the elders (cf. 14:23; 20:17–38). Thus, in this transitional moment, the elders along with the apostles bear responsibility for deciding the matter at hand.

Second, the council makes its deliberations on the basis of the divine economy of salvation—more specifically, on the basis of the prophetic-apostolic *interpretation* of that economy. Peter first presents the apostolic word to the council (15:7–11), a word that is confirmed when Barnabas and Paul bear testimony to the "signs and wonders God had done through them among the Gentiles" (15:12). James then presents the prophetic word to the council, articulating a hermeneutically rich tapestry of Old Testament quotations and allusions that anticipate God's visitation of the gentiles (15:13–18). On the basis of God's prophetic and apostolic Word, the council issues a "judgment" (15:19) that is deemed good by the apostles and elders (15:22), along with the Holy Spirit (15:28). Third, the council's judgment is formalized in a decree (Gk. *dogmata* in 16:4), the binding force of which is both to relieve the church from the burden of false teaching (15:10, 24, 28) and to preserve the church's freedom in the gospel of grace (15:11). It is this doubly binding function that in turn ministers encouragement, strength, and growth to the church (15:32; 16:4–5).

To the extent therefore that the church's dogmatic deliverances are indeed faithful summaries of the scope, shape, and substance of scriptural teaching, their use in interpretation does not constitute the imposition of an external burden or alien standard upon the interpreter of Holy Scripture. Church dogmas provide instead a divinely authorized interpretive key for unlocking the treasures of God's Word, a blessed pathway into Holy Scripture. In terms of more recent hermeneutical parlance, the rule of faith offers an entry point into the "hermeneutical spiral," that fruitful interplay of pre-understanding, reading, and growth in understanding that characterizes all acts of reading.[60]

59. Richard Bauckham, "James and the Jerusalem Church," in Richard Bauckham, ed., *The Book of Acts in Its Palestinian Setting* (Grand Rapids: Eerdmans, 1995), chap. 15.

60. Grant R. Osborne, *The Hermeneutical Spiral: A Comprehensive Introduction to Biblical Interpretation*, 2nd ed. (Downers Grove, IL: InterVarsity, 2006).

Though certainly not a matter of innate knowledge, the rule of faith functions for the Christian reader like a Kantian *a priori*: the rule of faith is not simply a truth that the interpreter thinks *about* when reading Holy Scripture; it is also a truth that the interpreter thinks *with* when reading Holy Scripture.[61] This at least is one of the ways that church dogmas and doctrines have functioned historically in biblical interpretation. Whether in Cyril of Alexandria's translation of the Nicene dogma into the directive that we read the Gospels in such a way that we ascribe every action and suffering of Jesus to one subject, the Word made flesh,[62] or whether in the Reformed and Lutheran confessional classification of the Word of God into the categories of "law" and "gospel,"[63] the rule of faith has functioned historically not only as a standard for measuring the faithfulness of one's exegetical results but also as a means for enabling the production of faithful exegetical results. According to Zacharias Ursinus, the "highest" purpose for studying church doctrine is to prepare us "for the reading, understanding, and exposition of the holy Scriptures. For as the doctrine of the catechism and Common Places are taken out of the Scriptures, and are directed by them as their rule, so they again lead us, as it were, by the hand to the Scriptures."[64]

Doctrinal pre-understanding enables reading. Nevertheless, doctrinal pre-understanding does not wholly determine the reading of a text before it is read. Such a scenario would actually foreclose the act of reading itself. For the reader of God's unfathomably rich Word, "There can . . . be no final act of reading in which everything is uncovered, in which the mine of gold has yielded all its treasure or the fish pool

---

61. Cf. George Lindbeck, *The Nature of Doctrine: Religion and Theology in a Postliberal Age* (Louisville: Westminster John Knox, 1984), 33.

62. See the "Third Letter of Cyril to Nestorius," *Anathema* 4, in Edward R. Hardy, ed., *Christology of the Later Fathers* (Louisville: Westminster John Knox, 1954), 353. See also Cyril's further elaboration of this point in his "Explanation of the Twelve Chapters," 12–14, in John McGuckin, *Saint Cyril of Alexandria and the Christological Controversy: Its History, Theology, and Texts* (Crestwood, NY: St. Vladimir's Seminary Press, 2004), 286–87.

63. Thus Zacharias Ursinus: "The chief and most important parts of the first principles of the doctrine of the church . . . may be divided . . . into the law and gospel" (*Commentary on the Heidelberg Catechism*, trans. G. W. Williard [1852; repr., Phillipsburg, NJ: Presbyterian & Reformed, 1985], 13).

64. Ursinus, *Commentary*, 10.

has been emptied of fish."[65] As Charles P. Arand states, "Dogma is no substitute for reading and studying the Scriptures themselves. . . . The purpose of dogma is to 'send us back into the Scriptures with more reader competence.'"[66] Furthermore, as Augustine recognized long ago, it is possible to arrive at an interpretation of Scripture that, though formally corresponding to the rule of faith, is nevertheless exegetically "mistaken."[67] The rule of faith does not obviate reading. Nor does it validate every orthodox reading.

These qualifications notwithstanding, the rule of faith offers a promising orientation or starting point for the reading of Scripture, an orientation within which our understanding of Scripture can grow. Moreover, because it summarizes scriptural teaching on God and God's unfolding economy of salvation, the rule of faith not only provides readers with a starting point for exegesis, it also identifies the goal of exegesis, which is to expound each particular text with an eye toward the broad horizons of scriptural teaching as a whole. In other words, the rule of faith serves as a benchmark for canonical exegesis. In this regard, the rule of faith also helps readers guard against a theologically reductionistic exegesis which would turn every text into the occasion for teaching a favorite doctrine—or for engaging a favorite controversy.

The question for the Christian interpreter therefore is not whether or not to read Holy Scripture in light of the rule of faith. The question is whether to read Holy Scripture with a right faith (i.e., orthodoxy), oriented toward the Triune God, drawn from the main contours of biblical teaching, and confessed by Scripture's faithful servant the church (cf. 1 Tim. 3:15), or whether to read Holy Scripture with a wrong faith (i.e., heterodoxy), drawn from some other purported source of wisdom and knowledge, and governed by the ends of some other community.[68] Reading Scripture in light of the rule of faith is a way of acknowledging that, when it comes to biblical interpretation, *sola Scriptura* (Scripture's status as the sole supreme authority for

65. Paul J. Griffiths, *Religious Reading: The Place of Reading in the Practice of Religion* (New York: Oxford University Press, 1999), 41.

66. Charles P. Arand, "The Church's Dogma and Biblical Theology," in Michael S. Horton, ed., *A Confessing Theology for Postmodern Times* (Wheaton: Crossway, 2000), 20.

67. Augustine, *On Christian Doctrine*, 533 (1.37.41).

68. Cf. Jenson, *Creed and Canon*, 81.

faith and life) cannot function appropriately as an interpretive norm apart from *tota Scriptura* (Scripture's teaching in its entirety). And Scripture's teaching in its entirety includes teaching about divinely authorized, subordinate authorities that have a role to play in biblical instruction and interpretation. The sacred script not only announces the saving drama that has unfolded "behind the text," it also directs the ecclesial drama that unfolds "in front of the text."[69] Reading Scripture in light of the rule of faith is also a way of acknowledging that submission to biblical authority is never a purely formal issue but always involves submission to Scripture's subject matter, supremely, the Triune Creator, Redeemer, and Consummator. As Herman Bavinck says, "Faith . . . reaches out in a single act to the person of Christ as well as to Scripture."[70] Reading Scripture in light of the rule of faith thus involves reading Scripture from within the context of our trinitarian faith, aided by the church's good confession, for the sake of the church's continuing growth in this trinitarian faith. To read Scripture in any other way is to read against the grain of its authority.

Conclusion

For all of the reasons outlined above, we should receive the rule of faith as part of the Spirit's rich bounty for the church, grateful that he has provided for us, in Holy Scripture, not only a supreme and authoritative fountain for our faith, but that he has also provided for us a confessional standpoint toward Scripture from which we may profitably draw upon Scripture's "pure spring of living water."[71] As Edmund Schlink states: "If the Confession is exposition of Scripture, that is, *doctrina evangelii*, a Confession, like all hearing and proclamation of the Gospel, does not result from human ability, but from the operation of the Holy Spirit who is given through Word and sacrament."[72]

---

69. This is one of the major theses of Vanhoozer, *Drama of Doctrine*.
70. Bavinck, *Reformed Dogmatics*, 1:569.
71. Ibid., 1:493.
72. Edmund Schlink, *Theology of the Lutheran Confessions* (Philadelphia: Fortress, 1961), 15.

5

In Defense of Proof Texting

The Indictment: Proof Texting in the Dock

Proof texting has been maligned as of late, charged in the court of theological inquiry. Many biblical scholars snicker and jeer its employment, while many systematic theologians avoid guilt by association. In this context, we wish to mount an argument *in defense* of proof texting. In so doing we claim neither to defend all that goes under the name of proof texting, nor to dismiss its critics' charges. Rather we argue that proof texting is not necessarily problematic; furthermore, historically it has served a wonderful function as a sign of disciplinary symbiosis among theology and exegesis.[1] We believe that a revived and renewed practice of proof texting may well serve as a sign of lively interaction between biblical commentary and Christian doctrine.[2]

This chapter was originally published in a slightly different form as "In Defense of Proof-Texting," *Journal of the Evangelical Theological Society* 54, no. 3 (September 2011): 589–606. Used by permission.

1. It is somewhat anachronistic to speak of disciplines of theology and exegesis when dealing with the classical theological tradition of the Western churches (say, in the time of Thomas Aquinas or John Calvin). Disciplines as such were a later development within university culture. But there were different literary genres written by theologian-exegetes, and dogmatics and commentary were clearly distinct genres.

2. For an earlier analysis of the perils and promise of "proof texting," see Daniel J. Treier, "Proof Text," in *The Dictionary for Theological Interpretation of Scripture*, ed. Kevin J. Vanhoozer (Grand Rapids: Baker Academic, 2005), 622–24.

Further, proof texting demonstrates the Reformed catholic nature of sound theology, in that it ties scriptural exegesis (attention to our final authority) to its context in the ongoing interpretative conversation of the communion of the saints as found in the exegetical tradition (our lesser authorities).

Two preliminary matters should be considered. First, insofar as we discuss "proof texting" or "proof texts," we employ a term in need of definition. Traditionally, "proof texts" (*dicta probanta*) were parenthetical references or footnote/endnote references to biblical passages that undergirded some doctrinal claim made, whether in a dogmatics textbook, a catechism, or a confession of faith.

Second, we should consider the way in which "proofs" were perceived to function in theology. What system of "warrant" underlies the practice of proof texting? The assumption behind proof texting, at least in classical Protestant theology, was not that the meaning of a cited proof text should be self-evident to the reader apart from the hard work of grammatical, historical, literary, and theological exegesis. Modern criticisms notwithstanding, classical Protestant theologians were not naive realists.[3] Rather, the assumption was that theology is a sacred science, whose "first principles" are revealed by God alone, and therefore that constructive theological argumentation must proceed on the basis of God's revealed truth, particularly as that revealed truth is communicated through individual passages of Holy Scripture, often understood as *sedes doctrinae* (that is, seats of doctrine).[4]

The Prosecution's Case

Our suggestion is counterintuitive for many or most readers, we imagine, and we wish to acknowledge the plethora of charges brought against proof texting as of late. Proof texting has been charged with three errors.

3. Carl R. Trueman, "It Ain't Necessarily So," *Westminster Theological Journal* 65 (2003): 311–25, esp. 314–15.

4. An early statement regarding this understanding of the Bible's role in theological science may be found in Clement of Alexandria, *Stromateis* 7.16.95 (*Alexandrian Christianity*, trans. John Ernest Leonard Oulton and Henry Chadwick, Library of Christian Classics [Philadelphia: Westminster, 1954], 154–55). See also Richard Muller, *Post-Reformation Reformed Dogmatics*, 2nd ed. (Grand Rapids: Baker, 2003), 2:518.

The first charge brought against the defendant is that *proof texting fails to honor the specific contexts of biblical texts*. In his essay "Approaches to New Testament Exegesis," Ralph P. Martin expresses dismay at what he calls the "dogmatic approach" to reading the Bible.[5] It does not honor the genre, historical setting, or literary texture of biblical texts. In Martin's words, this approach "sees it [the New Testament] as an arsenal of proof texts to be arranged, without much regard given to their literary form, historical context, theological purpose, or even their best translation into modern English, to form a network of probative evidence."[6] As the old adage has it, "a text without a context is a pretext for a proof text." The dogmatic approach of proof texting misunderstands the way meaning is conveyed: "The meaning of Scripture is atomized by being regarded as contained in key-words or key-phrases or isolated single verses treated without respect to their neighbouring context." By construing meaning as linked to discrete words or phrases, "little attention is paid to the teaching of the passage or book in which the individual texts appear."[7]

Martin sees a number of problems with this approach. First, "it misuses the text of Scripture by appealing to a truncated part (a verse) instead of the larger, more intelligible unit (a paragraph or longer section, according to the writer's purpose)." Second, "it cannot escape the charge of subjectivism when isolated verses are chosen because of their apparent suitability to 'prove a point.'"[8] Third, "it is forgetful of God's providence in conveying his word to men not in fragmented or situation-less dicta, but in the total context of the historical milieu of an ancient people (Israel, the early church) and through the medium of a set of languages which make use of non-prescriptive modes of expression." He suggests that "failure to recall this last point turns the New Testament into a legal code or a set of cold facts, like a telephone directory."[9] Consider this approach indicted.

5. Ralph P. Martin, "Approaches to New Testament Exegesis," in I. Howard Marshall, ed., *New Testament Interpretation: Essays on Principles and Methods* (Grand Rapids: Eerdmans, 1977), 220–21.

6. Ibid., 220.

7. Ibid.

8. Ibid.

9. Ibid., 221.

The second charge brought against the defendant is that proof texting too easily suggests that *doctrinal language is the biblical language
with no sensitivity for the horizon of the interpreter or the hermeneutical task involved in working with the biblical language*. In his essay
"The Voice and the Actor: A Dramatic Proposal about the Ministry
and Minstrelsy of Theology," Kevin Vanhoozer considers the claims of
Wayne Grudem's presidential address to the Evangelical Theological
Society in the year 2000.[10] In that address, entitled "Do We Act As If
We Really Believe that 'the Bible Alone, and the Bible in Its Entirety,
Is the Word of God Written'?" Grudem suggests that the way forward
for evangelical theology is to pursue "whole Bible exegesis."[11] What
does Grudem mean by "whole Bible exegesis"? He does not define it
precisely, though he gives examples (e.g., Craig Blomberg's *Neither
Poverty Nor Riches: A Biblical Theology of Possessions*, Jack Deere's
Surprised by the Power of the Spirit and Surprised by the Voice of God,
and D. A. Carson's *The Gagging of God*). The closest definition to
what such books do, in Grudem's words, comes earlier in the article:
"Not just what one verse says, or one book, but the whole of the Bible,
interpreted and applied rightly to the Church today."[12] Unfortunately
Grudem offers little help here in explaining what makes for right or
proper interpretation and application, beyond his insistence that it
take in the full panorama of biblical teaching (being not just New
Testament or Old Testament study, but "whole Bible" study).

To really grasp what is involved in interpreting and applying the
whole of the Bible to issues today, we must look to Grudem's own
Systematic Theology for some methodological clarity. He offers a
directive and then suggests three steps to achieve that goal. First, the
directive: "We should study systematic theology by collecting and understanding all the relevant passages of Scripture on any given topic."[13]

10. Kevin J. Vanhoozer, "The Voice and the Actor: A Dramatic Proposal about the
Ministry and Minstrelsy of Theology," in John G. Stackhouse, ed., *Evangelical Futures:
A Conversation on Theological Method* (Grand Rapids: Baker Books, 2000), 62–63.

11. Wayne Grudem, "Do We Act As If We Really Believe that 'the Bible Alone,
and the Bible in Its Entirety, Is the Word of God Written'?" *Journal of the Evangelical
Theological Society* 43, no. 1 (2000): 5–26.

12. Ibid., 7–8.

13. Wayne Grudem, *Systematic Theology: An Introduction to Biblical Doctrine*
(Grand Rapids: Zondervan, 2000), 35.

Second, he offers the three steps: "1. Find all the relevant verses. . . . 2. Read, make notes on, and try to summarize the points made in the relevant verses. . . . 3. Finally, the teachings of the various verses should be summarized into one or more points that the Bible affirms about that subject."[14] He does note that some verses may be pertinent even though they do not use particular words keyed to that topic, but the overwhelming push is to base systematic theology upon word studies. The theologian finds verses with words and phrases related to that topic across the biblical canon, by using a good concordance. Then they try to state each verse or section's teaching. Finally, they try to boil down these many summaries into a description of the whole Bible's message. In the end you have a doctrinal statement capped off with parenthetical references to texts that it summarizes.

In reply, Vanhoozer says that Grudem's method minimizes the Bible's deployment in theology, downplaying the systematic links between various topics of theology. In dealing with issues not directly addressed in Scripture, he asks, "Is it really the case that one can come to an appropriately theological understanding of birth control and gun control (to cite two of Grudem's dozen or so pressing problems) by exegeting the relevant portions of Scripture? Studying biblical words and concepts takes us only so far."[15] In other words, Grudem's approach does not honor the difference between biblical language and contemporary theological and ethical debates—it seems to elide any hermeneutical distance entirely.[16] Vanhoozer notes that we cannot overlook this difference: "It is one thing to know how a biblical author spoke or thought about a particular issue in the context of ancient Israel or the early church, quite another to relate those words and thoughts about a particular issue to the message of the

14. Ibid., 36.
15. Vanhoozer, "Voice and the Actor," 62.
16. It is also worth noting that this approach fails to distinguish between topics that the Bible directly and repeatedly speaks about (e.g., justification) and topics that the Bible only indirectly speaks about (e.g., gun control). The distinction is important to make because it determines the relative importance of general revelation for thinking about a particular topic, and it determines the way in which the Bible may be employed when addressing a particular topic (i.e., Does the Bible speak explicitly and at length to this topic, or does it sketch the lineaments of a worldview through which we may look at what general revelation reveals about this topic?).

Bible as a whole and to the significance of the Bible's teaching for us today."[17]

More recently, Vanhoozer has stated that proof texting flattens the biblical witness by overlooking the differences in genre and literary style.[18] In his words, "to force every biblical sentence into the same mold in a kind of 'one size fits all' hermeneutic is to read roughshod over the diverse literary genres of Scripture."[19] Vanhoozer also mentions that proof texting is not helpful in weighing biblical evidence for theological arguments. "Proof-texting assumes a uniform propositional revelation spread evenly throughout Scripture: one verse, one vote. Not only does this approach risk decontextualizing biblical discourse, it also leaves unclear just how the texts cited in support actually lend their support to the point in question."[20] Surely employment of narrative texts and biblical theological themes that permeate whole books or even collections of books (e.g., exile in the minor prophets) should play into a number of doctrines—yet these cannot always easily be referenced via word study or strict citation. In addition, poetic texts, parables, and Pauline letters all communicate in their own way, and it would be reductionistic to reduce them all to doctrinal verbiage. Such translation mistakes biblical language for contemporary dogmatics, when in fact they are distinct domains of discourse (and, yes, even Paul is not writing dogmatics per se).

The third charge brought against the defendant is that *proof texting interacts with ecclesiastical history rather than biblical history*. Recent years have seen scholars dismiss traditional readings of certain passages, claiming that their frequent employment in theological literature owes solely to ecclesiastical tradition and not at all to exegetical

---

17. Vanhoozer, "Voice and the Actor," 62–63.

18. Kevin J. Vanhoozer, *The Drama of Doctrine: A Canonical-Linguistic Approach to Christian Theology* (Louisville: Westminster John Knox, 2005), 270–72. We should mention that Vanhoozer himself practices—exemplifies even—the kind of proof texting that we call for (e.g., see n. 60 and all the parenthetical Scripture references in *The Drama of Doctrine*). But he consistently uses the term "proof texting" to refer to a misuse of the Bible—we think it can be applied in a more laudatory manner.

19. Vanhoozer, *Drama of Doctrine*, 270–71; cf. D. A. Carson, "Systematic Theology and Biblical Theology," in *New Dictionary of Biblical Theology*, ed. T. Desmond Alexander et al. (Downers Grove, IL: InterVarsity, 2000), 94–95.

20. Vanhoozer, *Drama of Doctrine*, 271.

rigor.[21] For example, a long tradition of theological work in the West has looked to Exodus 3:14 as a chief text shaping its doctrine of God, joining with other texts to suggest the holiness, transcendence, simplicity, and eternality of YHWH. God names himself, "I AM WHO I AM," and the Western theological tradition has routinely seen this to reveal a great deal about his character. Not so in much modern biblical studies. Martin Noth took the verse to delay naming of God.[22] In his recent commentary, Terence Fretheim argues against any metaphysical teaching in Exodus 3.[23] According to Jewish theologian Franz Rosenzweig, "all those who find here notions of 'being,' of 'the-one-who-is,' of 'the eternal,' are all Platonizing. . . . God calls himself not 'the-one-who-is' but 'the one-who-is-there,' i.e., there for you, there for you at this place, present to you, with you or rather coming toward you, toward you to help you."[24] Indeed it almost seems required now for exegetes to comment on the "Platonizing" or "Hellenizing" or downright "eisegetical" tendency to see Exodus 3:14 teaching anything about the character of God.[25] Exodus 3:14 has served as a proof text for "classical theism," but this says far more about the Hellenizing history of the early church and later traditionalism than it does about what God revealed at the burning bush to his servant Moses.[26]

In a common version of the present charge, and closely related to the first charge as well, critics accuse theologians of dislocating texts from their native literary and historical contexts in order to

21. Martin, "Approaches to New Testament Exegesis," 221.

22. Martin Noth, *Exodus: A Commentary*, trans. J. S. Bowden, Old Testament Library (Philadelphia: Westminster, 1962), 44–45.

23. Terence Fretheim, *Exodus: A Commentary*, Interpretation (Louisville: Westminster John Knox, 1991), 62–63.

24. Franz Rosenzweig, "A Letter to Martin Goldner," in Martin Buber and Franz Rosenzweig, *Scripture and Translation*, trans. Lawrence Rosenwald with Everett Fox (Bloomington: Indiana University Press, 1994), 191.

25. For example, see Christopher R. Seitz, *Figured Out: Typology and Providence in Christian Scripture* (Louisville: Westminster John Knox, 2001), 140; Richard Bauckham, *God Crucified: Monotheism and Christology in the New Testament* (Grand Rapids: Eerdmans, 1998), 78–79; George A. F. Knight, *Theology as Narration: A Commentary on the Book of Exodus* (Grand Rapids: Eerdmans, 1976), 23.

26. For further analysis of these charges and a rebuttal, see Michael Allen, "Exodus 3 after the Hellenization Thesis," *Journal of Theological Interpretation* 3, no. 2 (2009): 179–96; Michael Allen, "Exodus 3," in *Theological Commentary: Evangelical Essays*, ed. Michael Allen (London: T&T Clark, 2011), 25–40.

classify them according to the categories of dogmatic theology.[27] This anachronistic process, it is charged, inevitably distorts the meaning of Holy Scripture. D. A. Carson is a key representative of this criticism. According to Carson, dogmatic theology's desire to integrate biblical truth "into a *system*" determined by its own (often ahistorical and/or confessional) categories is more likely to distort or miss the meaning of God's multifaceted Word than the discipline of biblical theology, which is intrinsically more attentive to the distinctive historical and literary shape of the text and to its particular illocutionary emphases.[28] Indeed, for reasons such as this, some have recently wondered whether biblical theology might be capable of doing everything that systematic theology attempts to do—only better.

These charges amount to some major concerns: proof texting is dogmatic cherry-picking, an eisegetical use of the Bible, or ecclesiastical imposition on ancient literature.

The Cross-Examination of Evidence

We must acknowledge that the critics are on to something. All is not well in the house of systematic theology. With regard to the Bible in theology, we can speak of sins of omission and of commission.

Sins of Omission

Many note that the discipline has enjoyed a renaissance or revival in the last twenty to thirty years, especially in England. Whereas the 1960s were marked by "death of God theology" and the 1970s were known for the "myth of God incarnate," the last decade has been shaped by "Radical Orthodoxy."[29] Things sound more promising. While there are many blessings to note, no doubt, we must observe

27. Brevard S. Childs, *Biblical Theology of the Old and New Testaments: Theological Reflection on the Christian Bible* (Minneapolis: Fortress, 1993), 11.

28. Carson, "Systematic Theology and Biblical Theology," 94–95, 97, 101.

29. For those seeking introduction to the "Radical Orthodoxy" movement, see Michael Allen, "Putting Suspenders on the World: Radical Orthodoxy as a Post-Secular Theological Proposal or What Can Evangelicals Learn from Postmodern Christian Platonists," *Themelios* 31, no. 2 (2006): 40–53 (now available online: http://s3.amazonaws.com/tgc-documents/journal-issues/31.2_Allen.pdf).

that the growth of English systematic theology has not been stamped by and large by consistent exegetical concern. The major lights of this time period—Colin Gunton, John Webster, Rowan Williams, Bruce McCormack—have not (as of yet) engaged in lengthy commentary on the biblical text.[30]

Many systematic theologians have gained an appreciation for the importance of reading the Bible theologically, so much so that "theological interpretation of Scripture" is a growing academic discipline with its own journal, book series, dictionary, and so forth. Monographs seem to pour out with hermeneutical reflection on how to read the Bible. Yet one still looks in vain for books on various doctrinal topics that really tackle the task of theological exegesis at length. Furthermore, so many theological articles focus solely on relating to cultural theory, philosophical trends, or some realm of historical theology (with the Fathers, Puritans, and the post-Reformation era being among the most frequent sources these days). Above all, however, theologians focus on discussion of methodology—again, in conversation with philosophical, hermeneutical, historical, and even sociological resources. Many systematic theologians need to heed the words of ethicist Jeffrey Stout: "Preoccupation with method is like clearing your throat: it can go on for only so long before you lose your audience."[31]

This tendency has not simply occurred outside the realm of evangelical theology. Indeed Wayne Grudem has noted this temerity to engage the Bible in his assessment of contemporary evangelical theology. "For reasons I do not fully understand, within our lifetimes it seems to me a change has occurred whereby New Testament and Old Testament studies seem to the outsider to be so specialized that very few scholars outside those disciplines feel competent to interpret the Bible in any published article. They suffer from what we might call 'exegetophobia.'"[32] He made this assessment after surveying years of

30. It should be noted, though, that John Webster is currently preparing a commentary on the Epistle to the Ephesians and has prepared a number of shorter exegetical articles, and Rowan Williams is slated to write a commentary on Lamentations.
31. Jeffrey Stout, *Ethics after Babel: The Languages of Morals and Their Discontents* (Boston: Beacon, 1988), 163.
32. Grudem, "Do We Act As If?," 11.

journal articles and noting a trend whereby evangelical theologians interacted with secular sources and historical theology much more frequently than any biblical texts. We note his assessment simply to point out that evangelical theologians frequently fall into the same sin of omission that has plagued many other theological traditions— a disuse of explicit biblical argumentation in writings on Christian doctrine.

Sins of Commission

When they do engage the Bible, many systematic theologians have been guilty of misuse. There are narrow and wide examples of misuse.

We can consider a narrow misuse, that is, how one particular issue can be approached wrongly because of misunderstanding about how biblical passages lead to Christian doctrine. For example, John Feinberg, Robert Reymond, and Wayne Grudem express disagreement with the traditional doctrine of the "eternal generation" of the Son. If you analyze their arguments against eternal generation, they simply amount to exegesis of one key word.[33] Grudem is clear: "The controversy over the term 'only begotten' was unnecessary because it was based on a misunderstanding of the meaning of the Greek word *monogenēs* (used of Jesus in John 1:14, 18; 3:16, 18; and 1 John 4:19)."[34] Recent linguistic study has overturned the classical rendering of the word—"only begotten"—in favor of a newer translation: "one of a kind." Thus Jesus is called a unique son in these verses—not the singly begotten son. This parallels the usage of the term in Hebrews 11:17, wherein Isaac is *monogenēs* of Abraham (surely not his *only* son, for Ishmael was already on the scene). Grudem expresses frustration that the phrases "begotten of the Father before all worlds" and "begotten, not made" appear in the Nicene-Constantinopolitan Creed. The notion of "eternal begetting" is not necessarily contrary to the Bible, he

33. Unlike Reymond and Grudem, Feinberg also expresses some analytic concern for the idea of what could be conveyed logically by the doctrine of eternal generation—his argument, thus, is more wide ranging and less reductive (*No One Like Him: The Doctrine of God*, Foundations of Evangelical Theology [Wheaton: Crossway, 2001], 489).

34. Grudem, "Appendix 6: The *Monogenēs* Controversy: 'Only' or 'Only Begotten'?," in *Systematic Theology*, 1233.

says, but it is surely not required by the Bible. Indeed, he goes further: "Nothing in Scripture would indicate that we should affirm it."[35]

The approach exemplified by Grudem suggests that doctrines must be mandated by particular words or phrases. When a proof text—that is, a particular word seen to have dogmatic import—is no longer found to fill the role, the doctrine falls. In this framework, as Kevin Vanhoozer has shown, meaning is identified with terms and clauses as opposed to broader levels of communicative action. Furthermore, this kind of methodology fails to note that certain doctrines may derive from the conjoining of several biblical ideas rather than from explicit biblical warrant. In this case, patristic writers based the notion of eternal generation on the New Testament (especially the Johannine) presentation of the consistent pattern that characterizes the Father-Son relationship, a pattern exhibited in their common life *ad intra* (internally) and in their common work *ad extra* (externally),[36] as well as on other biblical analogies used to describe the Father-Son relationship (e.g., God-Word [John 1:1], Glory-Radiance [Heb. 1:3], etc.).[37] As another example, the so-called "covenant of redemption" (*pactum salutis*) was developed in the sixteenth and seventeenth centuries to express the eternal roots of the plan of salvation in the common life of the Trinity, something of a conjoining of the doctrines of election and Trinity.[38] Though there is no single text that stipulates the

35. Ibid., 1234.

36. Keith Johnson has demonstrated that Augustine's doctrine of eternal generation does not rest simply on his interpretation of *monogenēs*. For Augustine, the doctrine rests on the various ways in which the New Testament portrays the Father-Son relationship, including (1) the "sender-sent one" relationship (e.g., John 4:34; 5:23–24, 30–47; 6:38–44, 57; 7:16, 28–29, 33; 8:16–18, 26–29, 42; 9:4; 12:44–50; 13:16; 14:24; 15:21; 16:5, 28; 17:3, 18; 20:21); (2) the relationship between the Father as "giver" and the Son as "receiver," a relationship that obtains both in God's immanent life and in his external works (e.g., John 5:19, 22, 26, 27, 36; 10:18; 17:2, 8, 11, 22; 18:11); (3) the ordered unity of the Father and the Son in their works (e.g., John 1:3; 1 Cor. 8:6); (4) analogies between the Spirit's relationship to the Father (and the Son) and the Son's relationship to the Father (e.g., John 15:26; 16:13–14). See Keith Johnson, "Augustine, Eternal Generation, and Evangelical Trinitarianism," *Trinity Journal* 32 n.s. (2011): 141–63.

37. Thomas F. Torrance, *The Trinitarian Faith: The Evangelical Theology of the Ancient Catholic Church* (London: T&T Clark, 1995), 120–21.

38. Richard A. Muller, "Toward the *Pactum Salutis*: Locating the Origins of a Concept," *Mid-America Theological Journal* 18 (2008): 11–65; Carl Trueman, "From

existence of such a covenant, various texts imply the reality to which this covenantal language points.

We may also see wider misuse, wherein a whole theology can be justified by misleading standards about the use of the Bible in theology. Reviews of various theology texts can make much of mere references to texts, as if the quantity of references in and of itself demonstrates the biblical caliber of the theology. Such reviews frequently run free of analysis of the nature of such biblical reference, the contextual sensitivity of it, the way it makes good use of secondary scholarship (both classical and modern), and so forth.

Taking both errors of commission into account and acknowledging the frequent sin of omission, systematic theologians have much to which they must plead guilty as charged. Indeed the poor use of the Bible by theologians makes it far too easy for other charges to be brought against any and all "proof texting" in theology. We think this unfortunate, yet understandable. The burden of proof has shifted upon those, like ourselves, who would suggest that proof texting is a valid practice.

Is the Evidence beyond a Reasonable Doubt, or Is There Another Explanation?

Before discussing two models that might aid in recovering a positive understanding and use of proof texts, we should take note of one important fact: *All of the charges brought against proof texting in Christian theology could be lodged against the Bible's own use of the Bible.* With respect to the first charge: 2 Corinthians 6:16–18 cites and/or alludes to a litany of Old Testament passages (including Lev. 26:12; Isa. 52:11; 2 Sam. 7:14) in support of the claim that "we are the temple of the living God," but gives no indication of the distinct literary and historical contexts within which those passages are found. With respect to the second charge: Galatians 3:14 equates "the blessing of Abraham"—presumably the blessings of Genesis 12:3 and 15:6, which are cited in Galatians 3:6 and 3:8—with "the promised Spirit."

Calvin to Gillespie on Covenant: Mythological Excess or an Exercise in Doctrinal Development," *International Journal of Systematic Theology* 11, no. 4 (2009): 378–97.

However, the book of Genesis does not record any explicit promise regarding the Spirit's coming, a promise more clearly enunciated in much later prophetic texts (e.g., Joel 2:28; Isa. 44:3; 59:21). Here, then, we have an example of a text being used in a doctrinally more specific sense than its original context, taken by itself, allows. With respect to the third charge: Hebrews 1 collects a series of Old Testament texts, primarily from the Psalms, as witness to a single doctrinal theme, the Messiah's divine sonship. However, the deity of God's Son does not seem to be the main theological focus, if it is a focus at all, in any of these texts. Is the author of Hebrews allowing his own doctrinal interest, namely, establishing the deity of God's Son, to drive his collection and probative use of Scripture?

The reason for noting these examples is not to dismiss Scripture's use of Scripture. Nor is it to suggest that the apostles should be given a free hermeneutical pass when it comes to the use of proof texts because of their status as God's inspired spokespersons. The reason for drawing attention to these examples is to point out something now widely acknowledged by evangelical biblical scholars: namely, the use of Scripture by Scripture cannot be understood on the basis of citation techniques alone. To the contrary, if we are to appreciate the way Scripture uses Scripture to prove a doctrinal point, then we must appreciate the larger hermeneutical frameworks within which citations are employed, the original (historical and literary) contexts within which proof texts are found, and we must also possess a certain canonical sensitivity to how biblical motifs and themes unfold in the history of redemption, and, perhaps most importantly, how Christ is understood to be the climax of that unfolding historical development.[39] When such factors are acknowledged, the use of the Old Testament in the New Testament is much less open to the charge of arbitrary apologetics and appears to exhibit a more coherent hermeneutical procedure than initial appearances would have led us to appreciate.

What is the lesson to be drawn from this point? Simply this: we must not confuse citation techniques (e.g., proof texting) with hermeneutical method, whether we are considering Scripture's use of Scripture

39. A helpful collection of essays in support of this perspective, which also includes opposing views, may be found in G. K. Beale, ed., *The Right Doctrine from the Wrong Texts? Essays on the Use of the Old Testament in the New* (Grand Rapids: Baker, 1994).

or theology's use of Scripture. When it comes to the function of a proof text in a given theological argument, we should be willing to consider whether or not a particular usage of a text might make more sense to us if we considered the underlying hermeneutical rationale and the broader exegetical context that determined that particular usage. Our belief is that, if we did so, we would in many instances come out with a different appreciation of the function of proof texts in Christian theology than contemporary criticisms will admit. Our plea, then, is for consistency: let us extend to theology's use of Scripture the same patient and charitable attempt to understand that we extend to Scripture's use of Scripture's proofs. And let us not commit the fallacy of confusing a method of citation with a hermeneutical procedure. Indeed, if there is an immediate lesson to be drawn, it is this: proof texting (as a citation technique) has biblical precedent and therefore should not be too hastily dismissed.

While the charges are serious and are not without grounds, we suggest that things may not be as they seem. While the burden of proof is upon those who wish to employ proof texts, it can be demonstrated that this technique is neither necessarily unhealthy nor easily dispensable. Though systematic theologians nowadays may not carry a great deal of credibility with regard to their use of the Bible, we suggest that this is not logically necessary, nor has it traditionally been the case. In other words, things might be different and have, in fact, frequently been different. Perhaps there is another explanation for the role of proof texts in theology, and we believe a wider perspective is needed. By looking beyond our era of hyper-specialization, we can appreciate the way that proof texting served as a synthetic symbol of the coinherence of what John Webster calls "exegetical reasoning" and "dogmatic reasoning."[40] To that end we will consider the role of proof texts in the theological work of two theological giants from past centuries: Thomas Aquinas and John Calvin.

Thomas Aquinas is a hard man to characterize. He helped mediate disputes about the legacy of Aristotle within the arts faculty at the University of Paris, the preeminent educational institution of the

---

40. John Webster, "Biblical Reasoning," *Anglican Theological Review* 90, no. 4 (2008): 749–50.

day. He wrote four different systems of theology (his commentary on Peter Lombard's *Sentences*, the *Summa Contra Gentiles*, the *Summa Theologiae*, and the *Compendium Theologiae*—the last two were left unfinished). He participated in sizable ecumenical conversations with Eastern Christians on behalf of the papacy. Yet his day job was as master *sacra pagina* ("master of the sacred page"), a professor of biblical literature, giving lectures on various biblical books.

Thomas wrote commentaries and collected commentary. He left us commentaries upon Isaiah, Jeremiah, Job, John, Romans, Hebrews, and numerous other biblical texts. He collected the available patristic and medieval commentary upon the Synoptic Gospels in his *Catena Aurea*, something of a precursor to today's Ancient Christian Commentary on Scripture released by InterVarsity Press. Thomas did not see his various tasks as separated. While his work on Aristotle or angelology was distinguished from his thinking about Amos, it was never separated intellectually. In fact the work on philosophical theology and the history of doctrine was meant to shape his reading of Scripture. Of the thirty-eight thousand citations in the *Summa Contra Gentiles* and *Summa Theologiae*, over twenty-five thousand references come from Holy Scripture.

What role do these proof texts play in his theological argument? Thomas believes that *sacra doctrina* must flow from *sacra pagina*. He bluntly states: "When it comes to the things of God, man should not easily speak of them otherwise than does Sacred Scripture."[41] Scripture should guide theology.[42] We can see this principle shape the very form of argument in his theological masterpiece. In the question and answer format of the *Summa Theologiae*, Thomas raises a question, considers various answers from his opponents, lodges a contrary opinion, offers his own perspective, and then replies to each statement by his opponents. It is illuminating to see that the contrary opinions (*sed*

41. *Contra Errores Graecorum* 1.1.
42. For analysis of how Thomas uses the Bible in his theological work, see Wilhelmus Valkenberg, *Words of the Living God: Place and Function of Holy Scripture in the Theology of St. Thomas Aquinas*, Publications of the Thomas Instituut te Utrecht New Series 6 (Leuven: Peeters, 2000); Christopher Baglow, *"Modus et Forma": A New Approach to the Exegesis of Saint Thomas Aquinas with an Application to the "Lectura super Epistolam ad Ephesios,"* Analecta Biblica 149 (Rome: Biblical Institute Press, 2002).

contra: "on the other hand") tend to either quote Scripture or ecclesial authorities (especially Augustine). The decisive role and distinct shape of biblical proof texts not only points to the Bible's authority but manifests the way that Thomas makes use of a rich exegetical tradition in making such references. The quotation of a biblical passage in the *Summa* is meant to point the reader to a commentary written by Thomas or to an exegetical tradition of which he and the intelligent reader would be aware.

The *Summa* covers a wider terrain than any one biblical commentary—in fact, it could be characterized as a whole-Bible commentary with its very structure being shaped by what we now call "biblical theology."[43] The particular biblical commentaries contain more detailed expositions of pertinent passages that are merely referenced offhand or quoted briefly in the *Summa*. For example, he discusses the equality of power of the Father and of the Son in two types of texts (*Summa Theologiae* 1a.42.6 and in his *Commentary on John 5:19*). In the article in the *Summa Theologiae*, Thomas mentions a number of other texts in John's Gospel (5:20, 30; 14:31), and he makes reference to no patristic sources. When you trace those references or quotations to his commentary, however, you see extended analysis of a deep patristic tradition. He presents Hilary of Poitier's anti-Arian exegesis, as well as the interpretive approaches of Augustine, Didymus the Blind, and John Chrysostom. Gilles Emery summarizes: "One can see that the *Summa* organizes and summarizes the patristic teaching of the *Catena aurea* which the commentary on St. John (posterior in time) presents in greater detail. The commentary allows one to measure the deep patristic roots of the *Summa*'s doctrine on the subject of the equality of power of the Father and the Son."[44]

Sometimes he even mentions the exegetical tradition in his quotation. For example, he asks the question: "Besides the knowledge we have of God by natural reason is there in this life a deeper knowledge

43. Christopher T. Baglow, "Sacred Scripture and Sacred Doctrine in Saint Thomas Aquinas," in *Aquinas on Doctrine: A Critical Introduction*, ed. Thomas Weinandy, Daniel Keating, and John Yocum (London: T&T Clark, 2004), 11–14.
44. Gilles Emery, "Biblical Exegesis and the Speculative Doctrine of the Trinity in St. Thomas Aquinas's Commentary on St. John," in *Trinity in Aquinas* (Ypsilanti, MI: Sapientia, 2003), 306–7.

that we have through grace?" (1a.12.13).[45] Three answers are given, each of which boils down to the same answer: no. Then Thomas says: "On the other hand St. Paul says, *God has revealed to us through his Spirit,* a wisdom which *none of this world's rulers knew* and a gloss says that this refers to philosophers." The italicized words are biblical quotations from 1 Corinthians 2:8–10. Thomas not only refers to the biblical text, but he also makes reference to its history of interpretation. He concludes this sentence with a quotation from Jerome's gloss on 1 Corinthians 2, that is, Jerome's commentary upon the text as found within the lines of his Vulgate.[46] Thomas realizes that the gloss is an expansion or interpretation of the specific words of St. Paul—he finds this to be a plausible exegesis of the passage and references its primary or paradigmatic occurrence (in St. Jerome's work). Here a proof text serves to draw in not only an authoritative biblical passage, but its ecclesial interpretation as exemplified in the tradition. Thomas does not expand on all of the reasons for understanding "this world's rulers" as "philosophers," but he points to an authority who has done so. The quotation and the reference to Jerome serve as a footnote, so that the readers whose interest has been piqued at this point can trace the argument further back into a vibrant interpretive tradition.

John Calvin is another representative of the healthy relationship between exegesis and doctrine that has characterized much of the theological tradition. The sixteenth-century Genevan reformer is a particularly instructive example of the positive role that proof texts might play in theology because of the methodological sophistication he exhibits in distinguishing and relating the genres of biblical commentary and dogmatic theology.

Calvin's programmatic division of labor between exegesis and dogmatics grew in part out of frustration with the commentaries produced by some of his Protestant counterparts. In the dedication of his 1540 Romans commentary to Simon Grynaeus, Calvin faulted Melanchthon's approach to commentary writing for focusing too

45. Thomas Aquinas, *Summa Theologiae: Latin Text and English Translation, Introductions, Notes, Appendices, and Glossaries*, vol. 3, *Knowing and Naming God (1a.12–13)*, ed. and trans. Herbert McCabe (New York: McGraw-Hill, 1964), 43.

46. Jerome, *Missale Mixtum: Prefatione, Notis, et Appendicibus*, Patrologiae Latina 30, ed. J. P. Migne (Paris: 1862), 752.

exclusively upon select doctrinal points in the biblical text to the neglect of other textual issues and themes.[47] By failing to follow the discourse and argument of the text closely, and by focusing primarily upon issues of specific theological interest, this commentarial approach took the unacceptable risk of distracting readers from the message and intention of the biblical author. In the same dedicatory letter, Calvin also criticized Bullinger and Bucer for the method they employed in writing biblical commentary. Though their commentaries demonstrated greater commitment to tracing the flow of the text than did Melanchthon's, Calvin nevertheless found fault with their approach. In their commentaries, both theologians followed the (long-established) practice of capping the running commentary upon the text with long excurses on doctrinal *loci* which the text had either explicitly or implicitly mentioned.[48] This (to Calvin's mind cumbersome) practice also distracted readers from the rhetorical shape of the biblical text and thus represented a transgression of what he believed was the commentator's chief duty: to unfold with "lucid brevity" the mind of the author.[49]

Calvin's criticism was not that his contemporaries sought to elucidate dogmatic topics from the text of Scripture. For Calvin, like Aquinas before him, Scripture provided the foundation for all legitimate theological inquiry and was given by God to promote (among other things) specifically doctrinal ends. Calvin's criticism concerned the proper divisions that he believed should characterize theological labor. He believed that the work of elaborating upon the doctrinal *loci* revealed in Scripture, and of disputing relevant errors related to those *loci*, did not belong in the genre of biblical commentary because such discussions would distract the reader from the biblical author's particular argument and message. Instead, Calvin believed that the work of dogmatic exposition and disputation belonged in the genre of the *loci communes* ("common places"), a genre devoted

47. John Calvin, *The Epistle of Paul the Apostle to the Romans and to the Thessalonians*, Calvin's Commentaries, trans. Ross Mackenzie (Grand Rapids: Eerdmans, 1961), 2.

48. Richard Muller, *The Unaccommodated Calvin: Studies in the Foundation of a Theological Tradition* (New York: Oxford University Press, 2000), 28–29.

49. Calvin, *Romans*, 1.

to collecting and arranging in an orderly manner the common themes of Holy Scripture. Beginning with the 1539 edition of his *Institutes of the Christian Religion,* Calvin put this genre to great service in his theological program.[50]

While it is important to appreciate the distinction between biblical commentary and *loci communes* in Calvin's theological program, it is more important for present purposes to appreciate their relationship. The collection and orderly arrangement of topics into *loci communes* was a practice common to many academic disciplines in the sixteenth and seventeenth centuries.[51] It was not an exclusively theological genre. What was distinctive about the genre's usage in Protestant theology was its relationship to biblical exegesis.

The *loci communes,* as developed by Calvin and others, was dependent upon biblical exegesis in a number of important ways. Exegesis determined both the specific *topics* that were treated in the *loci communes* and also (in loose and varying ways) the *arrangement* of those topics. With respect to topics: the doctrinal themes treated in sixteenth- and seventeenth-century "common places" were not established by asking "what does the whole Bible say about *x?*" The topics treated in this genre were instead determined by the frequency with which they appeared in Holy Scripture—their status as truly *common* themes of the Bible—and also by the extent to which they were developed in certain foundational texts, or *sedes doctrinae.* For Calvin and his contemporaries, the Bible had a discrete message, speaking specifically about certain things and not about others, and it was the job of the *loci communes* to provide a reliable summary of this discrete message. With respect to arrangement, the topics treated in the *loci communes* were often arranged according to the Bible's unfolding historical economy of salvation,[52] or else according to some

50. See Elsie A. McKee, "Exegesis, Theology, and Development in Calvin's *Institutio*: A Methodological Suggestion," in *Probing the Reformed Tradition: Historical Studies in Honor of Edward A. Dowey, Jr.,* ed., Elsie A. McKee and Brian G. Armstrong (Louisville: Westminster/John Knox, 1989), 154–72; and especially Muller, *Unaccommodated Calvin.*

51. Joseph S. Freedman, "The Career and Writings of Bartholomew Keckermann (d. 1609)," *Proceedings of the American Philosophical Society* 141 (1997): 305–64.

52. Karl Barth, *Church Dogmatics,* vol. 4, *The Doctrine of Reconciliation,* part 1, ed. G. W. Bromiley and T. F. Torrance, trans. G. W. Bromiley (London: T&T Clark, 1956), 55.

other biblically derived order. In Melanchthon's and Calvin's cases, Paul's Epistle to the Romans provided a key, though not exclusive, organizational structure.[53] The ordering principle of the *loci communes* in early Protestant dogmatics was therefore neither "timeless" nor simply "logical," at least not in the senses that these terms are often used today.[54] The ordering principle in early Protestant examples of this genre reflected the theologian's intention to re-present in a faithful manner not only the Bible's distinctive content but also the Bible's distinctive shape in order to assist readers in understanding the biblical text.[55]

It only remains to be said that, when it comes to Calvin's *Institutes*, proof texts functioned as shorthand references to the more extended exegetical bases for doctrinal claims that could be found in his commentaries. As Richard Muller observes: "If one wishes to ascertain the biblical basis of Calvin's topical discussions and disputations, one *must* read the commentaries."[56]

We hope to have shown the common understanding of proof texts to be insufficient and to have proposed an alternative theory for how they may function in biblical and theological studies. We considered the way they serve as shorthand references in the works of Thomas Aquinas and John Calvin, leading readers of their dogmatic works to appropriate interpretive discussions in their commentaries or the commentary tradition they presupposed. For these theologians, proof texts did not subvert exegetical care—they symbolized and represented its necessity. Understanding the way that doctrines develop

53. See Muller, *Unaccommodated Calvin*, chap. 7.

54. It seems that many contemporary discussions of the differing organizational principles of biblical and systematic theology have confused what Johann Gabler said should be the case with what historically has been the case. This is an unfortunate (and anachronistic) oversight.

55. Consider Calvin's stated intention in writing the *Institutes*: "It has been my purpose in this labor to prepare and instruct candidates in sacred theology for the reading of the divine Word, in order that they may be able both to have easy access to it and to advance in it without stumbling. For I believe I have so embraced the sum of religion in all its parts, and have arranged it in such an order, that if anyone rightly grasps it, it will not be difficult for him to determine what he ought especially to seek in Scripture, and to what end he ought to relate its contents" (*Institutes of the Christian Religion*, trans. Ford Lewis Battles [Philadelphia: Westminster, 1960], 4).

56. Muller, *Unaccommodated Calvin*, 108.

out of and beyond the explicit statements in biblical texts is crucial for grasping the kind of claim made when one gives a proof text: it does not necessarily suggest that the doctrine as stated can be found there, but it does claim that the doctrine is rooted there in principle, when viewed in its larger canonical lens and when its implications are fully teased out.

Closing Arguments: Two Pleas to the Jury, One Final Analogy

What role will proof texting play in biblical and theological studies forthwith? The jury should consider two suggestions in assessing the future role, if any, of proof texts. We offer these proposals whereby proof texting need not be found guilty, but can be rehabilitated and may function as a wonderful sign of disciplinary symbiosis: theology and exegesis working hand in hand and side by side. We suggest some commitments from systematic theologians and others from biblical scholars.

First, systematic theologians must be aware of the burden of proof upon them to show that they are using the Bible well in their theological construction. They should seek to promote a biblically saturated culture among fellow evangelical systematic theologians.[57] We think they should realize that suspicion will remain upon them until this has been accomplished to some degree. But they should take cheer and remain hopeful, for history shows that theologians have been remarkable exegetes.

There are two ways in which to promote a biblically saturated culture among evangelical systematic theologians. First, engage in writing theological commentary (whether of whole books of the Bible or simply of particular passages in journal articles). Thankfully a number of avenues for such work have been birthed in recent years: commentary series, a journal, monograph series, and conference sessions focused on theological exegesis, theological commentary, and

57. See our reflections on the church as "creature of the Word" in "Guarding the Good Deposit: Dogmatic Tools for Thinking Scripture and Tradition Together" in chap. 3.

theological interpretation of Scripture.[58] More theologians should commit to an ongoing practice of doing exegetical work in their lectures, conference addresses, and their personal writing programs. Second, enrich dogmatic arguments with a great deal of exegetical excurses and engagement with works of exegetical and biblical-theological rigor. This is not simply to say that theologians should use the language of the Bible more.[59] One need not restrict oneself to using biblical terminology, but it would be surely strange to avoid using it or to use it less than, say, the jargon of modern philosophy or cultural theory.[60] More important than keeping familiar biblical terminology in play in systematic theology, however, is keeping faith with the duty to express the meaning of the Bible, and faithfulness to that calling cannot exist without lengthy, careful attention given to reflection on the shape of the canon and the study of particular verses.

Any hope of making headway in these directions will reshape the reading program of systematic theologians. Some careful consideration should be given to which journals are required reading, what monographs and texts must be devoured to attain competency, and, finally, what ways will most likely aid one's development as a dogmatic and an exegetical thinker. A regular practice of reading theologically interested biblical commentaries (both contemporary and classical) will likely fit in any such program, and we recommend that this be adopted by many theologians. There are institutional implications along these lines. We cannot assume that doctoral programs of the past prepared students well to do exegetically careful dogmatic theology. Too many top-notch programs will require more reading on Žižek than Zechariah or Zephaniah, more thinking about alterity than about the *imago Dei*. Without suggesting that we retreat from cultural engagement or reading of theology beyond the evangelical

---

58. For the lay of the land, see Daniel J. Treier, *Introducing Theological Interpretation of Scripture: Recovering a Christian Practice* (Grand Rapids: Baker Academic, 2008). See the brief survey provided in our introduction in this volume as well.

59. Rusty Reno, "Biblical Theology and Theological Exegesis," in Craig Bartholomew et al., eds., *Out of Egypt: Biblical Theology and Biblical Interpretation*, Scripture and Hermeneutics Series (Grand Rapids: Zondervan, 2004), 397.

60. John Webster has voiced this concern in various places over the years—perhaps most forcefully in a major review, "David F. Ford: Self and Salvation," *Scottish Journal of Theology* 54 (2001): 548–59.

pale, we do want to insist that priorities ought to be placed on the biblical writings and the classical dogmatic tradition of the orthodox churches. Of course there is another danger: some may have guided students into exegetical literature to such a degree that they have much less familiarity with historical theology and the shape of doctrinal development, involving issues in hermeneutics and the like.

Second, biblical scholars should expect rigorous exegesis to lie behind such proof texting and should engage it conversationally and not cynically. When reading an exegetical excursus or even a parenthetical reference within a dogmatic text, assume that it represents an attempt at teasing out valid implications from a portion of Scripture read in proper literary and canonical perspective. Remember that dogmatics does not merely remain within the explicit categories, much less the idiom of the Bible. Be open to implications being drawn from the conjoining of various biblical passages, even across literary divides (say, Pauline and Johannine letters, let alone the Synoptic Gospels). Belief in the divine authorship of Scripture feeds the analogy of faith (*analogia fidei*)—while every text must be read within its own immediate historical context, it cannot be restrained to that most narrow horizon but must be read within a broader canonical framework as well. Expect theologians to show how we move from texts and conglomerations of texts and themes eventually to biblical-theological movements and finally to constructive dogmatic assertions. Better yet, aid them in the endeavor by seeking to move beyond narrow exegetical arguments toward biblical-theological analysis in your own writing as a technical biblical scholar. The dangers of big-picture thinking being what they are (and anyone who tries or even watches carefully as others try knows how perilous the attempt can be), we will do well to have all hands on board as much as is practicable.

It might be helpful to point out that systematic theologians are not the only ones seeking to make use of organizing principles that are not always explicit in the Bible. Biblical theology also employs certain organizing principles and themes that function as systems or grids.[61] It is unfortunate, therefore, that some authors suggest that

---

61. Biblical theology, of course, takes different forms. It can operate as a narrative account of the history of revelation (e.g., G. Vos). It can function to offer a theology of particular biblical books or biblical authors (e.g., the New Testament Theology series

systematic theology imposes a foreign logic upon the Bible, while biblical theology more inductively follows the narrative shape of the Bible itself.[62] This is misleading for several reasons. The Bible itself is not a narrative. While it does tell a story of creation, fall, and redemption, it includes many elements and genres that cannot be classified as narrative, strictly speaking. Even Carson notes that biblical theology is a synthetic discipline that does not make use of all biblical materials but works selectively.[63] Moreover, the gospel—the best candidate for a "center" to Scripture—cannot be identified strictly with a narrative, for it includes not only the story of Jesus but also the application of that story to the spiritual well-being of persons throughout history (namely, Jesus's life, death, and resurrection bring about the "forgiveness of sins"). Furthermore, the Bible speaks about many relationships that are not strictly historical or temporal but that are more properly causal or "communicative"[64] (e.g., the relationship between God and the world [Rom. 11:33–36], the relationship between calling and conversion [John 6:44–45], etc.). Better to avoid claiming that either biblical theology or systematic theology is somehow closer to the Bible.[65] Instead, we can distinguish them by noting the types of organizing principles that each discipline draws from the Bible and expands in its own idiom. Biblical theology looks to narratival elements and construes its material in a diachronic, historically shaped format. Systematic theology actually makes wide use of this historical

---

published by Cambridge University Press). It can also trace themes through the Bible (e.g., many of the studies in the New Studies in Biblical Theology series published by InterVarsity Press, which trace the theme of the temple or race through the whole canon).

62. Carson, "Systematic Theology and Biblical Theology," 100–101.

63. Ibid., 91.

64. Cf. Kevin Vanhoozer, *Remythologizing Theology: Divine Action, Passion, and Authorship*, Cambridge Studies in Christian Doctrine (Cambridge: Cambridge University Press, 2010).

65. Geerhardus Vos was careful to eschew just such a claim in his inaugural address as Professor of Biblical Theology at Princeton Theological Seminary: "The very name Biblical Theology is frequently vaunted so as to imply a protest against the alleged un-Biblical character of Dogmatics. I desire to state most emphatically here, that there is nothing in the nature and aims of Biblical Theology to justify such an implication. . . . Dogmatic Theology is, when rightly cultivated, as truly a Biblical and as truly an inductive science as its younger sister" ("The Idea of Biblical Theology as a Science and as a Theological Discipline," in *Redemptive History and Biblical Interpretation*, ed. Richard B. Gaffin, Jr. [Phillipsburg, NJ: Presbyterian & Reformed, 1980], 23).

format (typically moving from God's life in eternity past to election to creation to fall to salvation in Christ to the application of that redemption now to the last things) and inserts other biblical concerns in various places (discussing repentance under the application of redemption, even though repentance was necessary both before and after the coming of Jesus, temporally considered).[66] Whereas biblical theology fixes narrowly upon the history of redemption, systematic theology moves beyond (though not around) this to also consider the way this history of salvation (*historia salutis*) is applied to persons (*ordo salutis*).[67]

Along these lines, biblical scholars will do well to familiarize themselves with the history of biblical interpretation. They will begin to see how dogmatics and exegesis can function in harmony, each enriching the other with diverse gifts.[68] By reading the commentaries of Calvin alongside his *Institutes* or by dipping into the expository homilies of Augustine on 1 John or Genesis, they will see how the church has always insisted on teasing out doctrinal implications from interpretive insights.

If both concerns are honored, proof texts could be a literary signal of a disciplinary symbiosis and of Reformed catholicity. They could serve once again to highlight the necessary interpenetration of exegesis and dogmatics. Still further, they could be a means through which the catholic reception of the Bible's teaching is passed along and made part of the exegetical work of each generation of scribes in the church.

---

66. It is too frequently overlooked that systematic theologies (like ecumenical creeds) tend to be structured based on biblical patterns or histories (whether the descent/ascent theme of New Testament Christology that guides the Nicene-Constantinopolitan Creed or the exit/return motif from the Old Testament that shaped Thomas Aquinas's *Summa Theologiae*). While systematic theology is not limited to the historical framework, it typically begins there in its organizational principles (contra Carson, "Systematic Theology and Biblical Theology," 95).

67. Instructive regarding the relationship of the *historia salutis* and *ordo salutis* is Richard Gaffin, *By Faith, Not By Sight: Paul and the Order of Salvation* (Milton Keynes, UK: Paternoster, 2006).

68. In particular note the ecclesiastical reflections on how creeds and confessions are meant to serve and shape exegesis in chap. 4.

AFTERWORD

Rediscovering the Catholic-Reformed Tradition for Today

A Biblical, Christ-Centered Vision for Church Renewal

J. Todd Billings

The dominant, operative theologies of Christians in the contemporary West are neither biblical nor Christ-centered; whether one considers revivalistic evangelicalism, confessional Protestantism, mainline Protestantism, or Roman Catholicism, sociological research shows that adherents increasingly reflect a shared theology that is a deformity of their particular traditions. "Christianity is actively

This chapter was originally published in a slightly different form as "Catholic and Reformed: Rediscovering a Tradition," *Pro Ecclesia* 23, no. 2 (2014): 132–46. It is a revised version of a lecture delivered on April 17, 2013, for the inauguration celebration of the Gordon H. Girod Research Professor of Reformed Theology at Western Theological Seminary. Particular thanks go to the donors who made this research chair possible.

being colonized and displaced by a quite different religious faith," as Christian Smith and Melinda Lundquist Denton have argued.[1] In many ways, in this colonizing theology, the religious consumer has become king; the God of Israel, made known in Jesus Christ, is only confessed when it fits into the consumer's own sovereign plans for what a deity can and cannot be. If the Bible, or the historic Christian tradition, holds a teaching that leaves the religious consumer with a sour taste, it can be jettisoned. This internalizes a message that has become ubiquitous in the late modern West: our lives—especially our "religious lives"—are our own private affairs to manage.

This essay explores an issue at the intersection of doctrine, congregational ministry, and contemporary culture: how to respond to this colonizing, cultural theology with a theological and ecclesial vision that is both catholic and Reformed. In this way, I supplement the dogmatic and historical work in the earlier chapters of *Reformed Catholicity* by sketching how a catholic and Reformed vision has promise in responding to this contemporary challenge in a way that rediscovers a biblical, Christ-centered path toward church renewal. There are various recent proposals that seek to respond to the theological and ecclesial decline that has marginalized a biblical, Christ-centered vision. While these proposals are offered with good intentions, I believe that some of them actually deepen the problem rather than lead toward genuine renewal. Many of these approaches, on the ecclesial right and the left, seek to "reinvent" the church, or unearth a "revolutionary" Jesus in a way that ultimately reinforces the contemporary cultural captivity that they seek to overcome. In contrast, an approach that is both catholic and Reformed challenges the deep and often hidden assumptions that place the religious consumer in the center, and the drama of the Triune God on the sidelines. It opens up a place for ecclesial life and theological reflection that is wide and spacious, yet specified in its worship of the Triune God and rooted in theological conviction. It gives a path toward church renewal in which our consumer priorities are gradually displaced by the Spirit as we are incorporated into Christ and his corporate body, fed at the

---

1. Christian Smith with Melinda Lundquist Denton, *Soul Searching: The Religious and Spiritual Lives of Emerging Adults* (New York: Oxford University Press, 2005), 171.

Pulpit and the Table as adopted children of the Father. Our stories as religious consumers are incorporated into the dying and rising of Christ by the Spirit—for our life is found in Christ and union with him. "For you died, and your life is now hidden with Christ in God. When Christ, who is your life, appears, then you also will appear with him in glory" (Col. 3:3–4 NIV).

A Tale of Two Creeds

I begin with a word from the Heidelberg Catechism that displays the biblical, Christ-centered vision that is central for a catholic-Reformed identity:

Q. What is your only comfort in life and in death?

A. That I am not my own, but belong—body and soul, in life and in death—to my faithful Savior, Jesus Christ.

He has fully paid for all my sins with his precious blood, and has set me free from the tyranny of the devil. He also watches over me in such a way that not a hair can fall from my head without the will of my Father in heaven; in fact, all things must work together for my salvation.
Because I belong to him, Christ, by his Holy Spirit, assures me of eternal life and makes me wholeheartedly willing and ready from now on to live for him.[2]

There is nothing remotely all-American about this statement: its starting point is *displacement*—I am not my own, but belong to Jesus Christ, to whom I have been united by the Spirit. This displacement is central to Christian identity, for as Jesus says in Mark's Gospel, "Whoever wants to be my disciple must deny themselves and take up their cross, and follow me. For whoever wants to save their life will lose it, but whoever loses their life for me and for the gospel will save it" (Mark 8:34–35 NIV). Instead of myself and my own interests, the Heidelberg sees the active, saving Triune God at the center

2. "The Heidelberg Catechism," in *Our Faith: Ecumenical Creeds, Reformed Confessions, and Other Resources* (Grand Rapids: Faith Alive, 2013), 69–70 (Q and A 1).

of the drama. As Christians, we inhabit a world in which we are adopted children of a gracious Father who is at work in the world, and anointed with the Holy Spirit who assures us that this union with Christ will never end, and empowers us for service to God, for the sake of Christ's kingdom—loving God and neighbor. All of this is enabled for sinners like us by Jesus Christ, who is the victor over sin and the devil. In many ways, the rest of the Heidelberg Catechism is an exposition of the vision concisely exposited here: it is God-centered, Christ-centered, deeply biblical, serious about our sin, and serious about our redemption.

In order to see how deeply countercultural this vision from the Heidelberg Catechism is, we should consider another, more recent, creed. This creed is *not* about displacement to find our life in Christ rather than ourselves. This is the "creed" of Moralistic Therapeutic Deism (MTD)—a widespread set of core beliefs, described by the most comprehensive study ever conducted on the beliefs of American youth. Yet, as further study has shown, the beliefs of youth largely reflect those of their elders.[3]

The MTD creed is this:

1. A God exists who created and orders the world and watches over human life on earth.
2. God wants people to be good, nice, and fair to each other, as taught in the Bible and by most world religions.
3. The central goal of life is to be happy and to feel good about oneself.
4. God does not need to be particularly involved in one's life except when God is needed to resolve a problem.
5. Good people go to heaven when they die.[4]

The contrasts between this and the Heidelberg are legion, but for the sake of this essay, I will name just a few to help explain the

3. Christian Smith with Kari Christoffersen, Hilary Davidson, and Patricia Snell Herzog, *Lost in Transition: The Dark Side of Emerging Adulthood* (New York: Oxford University Press, 2011), 11–13.
4. Smith with Denton, *Soul Searching*, 162–63.

threefold name of MTD: the purpose of religion, here, is "moral-istic"—it is to "be good, nice, and fair to each other." Unlike the Heidelberg, this is not set in the context of sin. There is no sense, here, that we are alienated from God on our own and thus need a mediator (Jesus Christ), or divine empowerment to do good (the Holy Spirit). Instead, religion is the sort of thing that tells us to try hard to "be good, nice, and fair"—something fully within our power. Why should we be good, nice, and fair? Because it fits the overall goal of religion, the T (Therapeutic) of MTD: "to be happy and to feel good about oneself." The central actor in this drama is the trinity of me, myself, and I—religion is about the individual. The self is not displaced—to the contrary, religion is here to build up my self-esteem or it's not doing its job. I am ultimately my own. Who is the God of MTD? Well, if religion is moralistic, but we don't need God's help to be moral, and if religion is to make us feel good about ourselves, then it makes sense that we end up with D, a deistic God: a God who created the world but left it to run on its own, a God "who does not need to be particularly involved in one's life except when God is needed to resolve a problem."

Along with Christian Smith, I sense that an MTD vision has pen-etrated our culture, as well as our institutions and our churches. In many ways, it has become the shared, operational cultural theology for a diverse range of both Christian and non-Christian Americans. But rather than multiply examples, for the purpose of this essay I want to supplement this portrait with an insight from Princeton sociologist Robert Wuthnow about a practice that undergirds MTD. According to Wuthnow, "religious tinkering" has become a wide-spread religious practice, especially among twenty-somethings and thirty-somethings.[5] Religious tinkerers pick and choose from the Bible and from other sources to find what solves their problems, what fills their needs and makes them happy. MTD already puts the individual and their own happiness at the center of faith. This logi-cally leads to the practice of religious tinkering. In the words from Elizabeth Gilbert's best-selling *Eat, Pray, Love*: "You have every right

5. Robert Wuthnow, *After the Baby Boomers: How Twenty- and Thirty-Somethings Are Shaping the Future of American Religion* (Princeton: Princeton University Press, 2007), 14–16.

to cherry-pick when it comes to moving your spirit and finding your peace in God."[6]

When we compare these two approaches, it is clear that the widespread functional theology of MTD is neither biblical nor Christ-centered. It is distant from the catholic-Reformed approach to Christian identity reflected in Heidelberg Catechism Q and A 1—that "I am not my own" but "belong" to Jesus Christ. I think that many observers would agree that MTD constitutes a crisis for the Western church, and that if the church in general and congregations in particular are to experience renewal, they need a substantial *alternative* to MTD.

Moreover, as the subtitle of this essay indicates, I think that a path out of MTD toward church renewal will involve moving toward a biblical, Christ-centered vision. But what does that really mean? Many today *claim* to be biblical and Christ-centered. But there is *more than one way* to seek to be biblical and Christ-centered. Below I note a few brief, popular-level attempts to be biblical and Christ-centered that I think are ultimately counterproductive: whether from the ecclesial right or the ecclesial left, they are actually promoting forms of the faith that functionally support and deepen MTD. After that, I move on to describe how a vision that rediscovers the catholic-Reformed tradition—with resources like the Heidelberg Catechism—presents a true alternative to an MTD approach to the faith. The final section of my essay gives a sketch of what it means to be catholic and Reformed today—both on a congregational level, and in terms of a theological program for further research.

Modern Evangelical and Progressive Correlationist Approaches

For many, seeking to be Christ-centered means getting back behind the church, which is peripheral and distracting, if not downright duplicitous. With these approaches, only the most ancient "original meaning" (i.e., "primitive meaning") of the Bible matters—so contemporary readers should do a *leap* over history and the history of interpretation. Why? Because interpreting the Bible is largely about digging through

6. Elizabeth Gilbert, *Eat, Pray, Love* (New York: Penguin Books, 2006), 208.

the rubble of mistaken "tradition" to find the true meaning, which "the church" has been hiding. We can see this approach in emergent church voices such as Brian McLaren in *The Secret Message of Jesus*. The book's project is guided by archaeological imagery: it is one of "excavation," "digging beneath the surface to uncover Jesus's message,"[7] "pealing back the layers of theology and history, seeking to find the core of Jesus's message,"[8] and uncovering that which church tradition has obscured: "For centuries at a time in too many places to count, the Christian religion has downplayed, misconstrued, or forgotten the secret message of Jesus entirely,"[9] McLaren writes. Of course, McLaren thinks *he* has now found the "secret message of Jesus." But he displays a great deal of suspicion toward the quests of others.

This primitivist, archaeological approach is also displayed in more "conservative" or "evangelical" authors, such as Alan Hirsch. Hirsch has repeatedly argued for a quite novel interpretation of Ephesians 4:11 as teaching a "fivefold" ministry that is absolutely foundational for the church. In his recent book on the subject, *The Permanent Revolution*, coauthored with Tim Catchim, he shows us what is at stake in this primitivism. They admit that no one advocated this reading of Ephesians 4 before the twentieth century, and that out of the "many millions of theological books that have ever been written, we cannot find serious exploration of the topic of fivefold ministry as a living and vital piece of the church's genetic codes"[10]—which is, in their view, the truly biblical approach. "How can we explain this? . . . The only conclusion we can reach is that this must ultimately be the work of the Devil."[11] They go on to explain how the devil has made the historic church ineffective in its ministry through adopting a false interpretation of Ephesians 4 rather than adopting their own interpretation. Do you disagree with their interpretation of the most "primitive" meaning of the text? Well, then, the hermeneutic of suspicion returns—you must be under the influence of satanic deception.

7. Brian McLaren, *The Secret Message of Jesus: Uncovering the Truth that Could Change Everything* (Nashville: Thomas Nelson, 2006), 1.

8. Ibid., 26.

9. Ibid., 78.

10. Alan Hirsch and Tim Catchim, *The Permanent Revolution: Apostolic Imagination and Practice for the 21st Century Church* (San Francisco: Jossey-Bass, 2012), 6.

11. Ibid.

Although the rhetoric of Hirsch and Catchim is extreme, their logic of primitivism is actually quite common in evangelicalism today: a new interpretation of the Bible that flies in the face of the history of interpretation is often seen as evidence *for* the novel position rather than evidence against it.

Indeed, similar rhetoric is used from time to time by leading biblical theologians today, such as in the title of a major lecture by N. T. Wright: "How God Became King: How We've All Misunderstood the Gospels."[12] While there is much in Wright's corpus of writing that can combat the assumptions of MTD, such rhetoric actually reinforces key aspects of the individualistic, tinkering approach to Scripture that sees novelty as a sign of veracity: implied in the subtitle is that "we've all misunderstood the Gospels until *I* illuminate them for you now." The history of interpretation—and interpretations in contemporary communities of faith—are being corrected by the bold, individual biblical scholar.

Not surprisingly, the Christ who emerges from primitivist accounts is often one who is "misunderstood" by the tradition, a kind of "revolutionary" whose bold vision was never fully realized. Browsing the stacks of Christian bookstores, one can find books of various ideological directions which cast Jesus in these terms: some books ask us to go "to the side of the Rebel Jesus,"[13] which involves embracing a left-wing social and political agenda; others read Jesus, and the Bible as a whole, in light of so-called "conservative" values, as in the bestselling *American Patriot's Bible*.[14]

These approaches are what I call "correlationist" in their theological method: they start with our own cultural agenda, questions, and needs, and then *correlate* an answer from the Bible in those terms. Without a doubt, the Jesuses emerging from these correlationist interpretations of Scripture are *relevant*. We dig through—or simply bypass—our

12. Lecture title for his "January Series" lecture at Calvin College in 2012. See http://www.calvin.edu/january/2012/NTWright.htm. Wright's book title on this subject is only a minor improvement on this rhetoric: *How God Became King: The Forgotten Story of the Gospels* (New York: HarperOne, 2012).

13. Brian D. McLaren, *Everything Must Change: When the World's Biggest Problems and Jesus' Good News Collide* (Nashville: Thomas Nelson, 2007), 227–36.

14. Richard Lee, ed., *The American Patriot's Bible: The Word of God and the Shaping of America* (Nashville: Thomas Nelson: 2009).

exegetical and theological traditions in response to Scripture in order to interpret it in a way that answers *our* questions: How can Jesus help us solve global political problems? How is Jesus significant for the founding of our nation, and the establishment of conservative values? In the end, however, these approaches reflect a cultural captivity that moves away from the gospel. Rather than seeing the paradigm for biblical interpretation in the celebration of Word and Sacrament— as part of a communal journey by the Spirit toward conformity to Jesus Christ—it reduces interpretation to individual acts of historical judgments in which our pressing questions set the agenda; in doing so, it fails to recognize the true context for interpreting the Bible as Scripture—as disciples united to Christ by the Spirit, listening for a word that will transform God's people into Christ's image for service and mission. Correlationist approaches seek to be biblical and Christ-centered. But approaches on the left and the right end up funding aspects of MTD; instead of starting with the displacement of the self by reading as ones who belong to Christ, they seek out a relevant Jesus that accommodates "me-centered religion," or they adopt a historical method that champions the "tinkering" judgment of the individual. Both need to absorb this phrase from the Heidelberg Catechism much more deeply into their prolegomena: "I am not my own, but belong . . . to my faithful Savior, Jesus Christ."

The Catholic-Reformed Tradition as Corrective

In contrast, the catholic-Reformed tradition offers a substantive alternative—both to MTD and to today's correlationist approaches.

Rather than starting with the individual who "jumps over" history to read the Bible, a key Reformed conviction about Scripture is displayed in its function: in the communal proclamation of Scripture through Word and Sacrament, believers are nourished by Jesus Christ through the Holy Spirit. In addition, from a formal standpoint, the exegesis of Scripture provides the material basis for catholic-Reformed theology. Scripture has a higher authority than tradition, and tradition is always revisable in light of the teaching of Scripture; however, that does *not* mean that the catholic-Reformed approach eschews tradition in approaching Scripture. To the contrary, Scripture fits within the broader matrix of God's redemptive work among his people. Scripture is God's chosen means used in uniting his people to Christ by the Spirit and enabling their conformity to Christ as children of the Father. In contrast to certain primitivist and archaeological approaches, the catholic-Reformed tradition does not attempt to approach Scripture as a "blank slate," but actually privileges trinitarian and christological convictions to help show us *how* to approach the Bible as *Scripture*. The catholic-Reformed tradition also seeks to read Scripture with Christians of other ages, recognizing the Spirit's work in the past. Doing so helps our cultural idols of the present to be exposed as we seek to be receptive to the Spirit's Word culminated in Christ in the Scriptures. In contrast to a correlationist approach, the catholic-Reformed tradition does not read the Bible as the source for answering *our* questions, and thus fitting into our own cultural agenda: instead, we receive Scripture as disciples who, by the Spirit, are having our own cultural idols and priorities *displaced*. We "are not our own," but we read Scripture as those who belong to Jesus Christ.

This means that being Christ-centered is not just about finding a "relevant" Jesus, but about losing our lives for Christ's sake. In its Christology, the catholic-Reformed tradition is *catholic*—such that it gives a trinitarian (Nicene) account that holds to the cosmic centrality of Jesus Christ as the mediator between Creator and creation (Chalcedonian). It also emphasizes both gifts received in union with Christ: the acquittal and pardon received through justification, and the new life of sanctification received by the Spirit, being sent for service and mission in the world.

Rather than privileging the questions of the present cultural moment and correlating them to the Bible, a theology of retrieval patiently and creatively attends to the texts and traditions of earlier ages, appreciative of the Spirit's work in the past. As it does so, it does not simply seek to "repristinate" the past into the present. Rather, it seeks to allow these voices and practices to reveal the blind spots and overcome the hidden idolatries of the present as it submits to Scripture as the Spirit's Word to conform us to Christ. The retrieval of postbiblical tradition is *culminated*, then, in the act of hearing the living God's address anew through Scripture, not vice versa. This retrieval, and the scriptural interpretation that it climaxes in, is "biblical" and

"Christ-centered" in a way that involves seeing with new eyes, and overcoming the fixation with the "new," the "relevant," and the "plausible" according to our present culture.

In light of MTD and the challenges of the need for renewal in today's church, much of what is missing in the correlationist attempts to be "biblical" and "Christ-centered" is a catholic sensibility and a catholic-Reformed sense of the breadth and depth of a dynamic, biblical tradition. But why do I use the term "catholic"? In a basic sense, I refer to our confession of "the holy catholic church" in the Apostles' Creed—a church that is catholic and universal, not by what it has done, but by its God-given identity of oneness in Christ, rooted in the teaching of the apostles. By using the term "catholic-Reformed," I am suggesting that being Reformed is not an autonomous end in itself, but is a way to occupy the "holy catholic church." I sometimes describe this dynamic in terms of an underground water table: many American Christians today think that they do not have to occupy any particular tradition, but can pick and choose from many traditions—like digging a hole here and there looking for water. But when one learns to really inhabit a tradition with depth, one can hit the "catholic water table." At that point, Baptists, Pentecostals, Roman Catholics, Reformed, and Orthodox can all find areas of common ground, even amid real and significant ongoing differences.

But some may wonder—is the "catholic-Reformed tradition" something that I made up? Are there churches today that occupy this tradition? No, I did not make it up, and yes, there are catholic-Reformed churches today. First, I will focus upon some historic examples of the tradition.

In the sixteenth and seventeenth centuries, Reformed theologians self-consciously regarded themselves as "catholic"—they claimed church fathers such as Augustine as their own; moreover, they saw themselves belonging to the tradition of the great early ecumenical creeds. The Belgic Confession gives a superb example of this: its doctrine of God, the Trinity, and Christ draws deeply upon patristic theology and early ecumenical statements of doctrine. In its significant attention to the sacraments, prayer, and worship, it continues the broadly catholic concern of making these practices central to Christian identity, even as it revises aspects of Roman Catholic doctrine on these points. But the Belgic is also clear about its Protestant identity—on salvation, Scripture, the sacraments, and related topics, it is unmistakably Protestant. This pattern—of drawing upon patristic along with medieval theologians while making fruitful use of the history of biblical exegesis—continued to be a strong pattern in the Reformed tradition for centuries. Thus, it is not surprising that Reformed scholastics continued to develop catholic instincts in their work; for example, William Perkins titled one of his works *A Reformed Catholike* (1597), and movements such as the Dutch "Second Reformation" drew deeply upon medieval theologians such as Bernard of Clairvaux. It should not surprise us that in the nineteenth century, it was a scholar in the German Reformed tradition, Philip Schaff, who undertook the massive project of first editing and publishing an English translation of the Ante-Nicene, Nicene, and Post-Nicene church fathers. Schaff's colleague at Mercersburg Seminary, John Williamson Nevin, shared an interest in both the church fathers and a reappraisal of Calvin and the Reformed Confessions; this led Nevin to propose a deeply catholic—and yet distinctively Reformed—theology of the incarnation and the Lord's Supper that shaped his theology of the church. It should not surprise us that at the turn of the twentieth century, a central figure in Dutch Reformed theology, Herman Bavinck, drew deeply upon the church fathers and medieval doctors in his four-volume *Reformed Dogmatics*—in critical yet appreciative appropriation. Also in the Dutch Reformed tradition, a central advocate of mid-twentieth-century Reformed liturgical renewal was a Mercersburg scholar (Howard Hageman), who speaks of the Reformed tradition as "the Catholic Church, Reformed." Indeed, as Hageman argues, the Reformed tradition does not claim to "restore" a church that had eclipsed, but to reform the historic catholic church, for even "the very name 'Reformed' implies continuity. A tree which is reformed is not cut down; it is pruned. Just so with our church; one with the historic church of Jesus Christ, it has been purified and restored by that keenest of all instruments, the living Word of God."[15] Thus, it was with great precedent that John Hesselink, in his inau-

---

15. Howard Hageman, *Our Reformed Church* (Grand Rapids: Reformed Church Press, 1995), 1.

gural presidential address at Western Theological Seminary in 1973, used three words in naming the mission of the Reformed Church in America's seminary: "Catholic, Evangelical, and Reformed."[16] All of this is just a very small sampling of the long tradition of articulating a Christian identity as both Reformed and catholic. Some would rather speak of "ecumenical" here than "catholic"; but I sense that to replace the term "catholic" with "ecumenical" would involve a significant loss, since the contemporary ecumenical movement represents some instincts that are catholic and some that are not, in this older sense of the term. Today, theologians such as Kevin Vanhoozer, James K. A. Smith, and the authors of this volume are seeking to revive the use of this older sense of the term of being "catholic" and evangelical, "catholic" and Reformed—with a prominent example of this pairing displayed in a recently announced fifteen-volume New Studies in Dogmatics series, published by Zondervan Academic. As one of the series editors, Michael Allen describes in a press release, "We believe that the way to *renewal* is through *retrieval* of our catholic and Reformational heritage."[17]

Living Out a Catholic-Reformed Faith

So, is a catholic-Reformed tradition just an abstraction from the ivory tower, or does it have real-life implications for congregations today? I believe that—as a pathway to church renewal—it does have real-life implications, even if some of the routes that I will describe at the end of the essay are scholarly ones for working toward church renewal. Before that, let us explore the congregational implications by comparing two relatively well-known churches: Willow Creek Community Church in South Barrington, Illinois, with its lead pastor Bill Hybels, and City Church of San Francisco, a large and growing urban congregation. Both churches would be considered broadly "evangelical" but, in many ways, Willow Creek, and the seeker-sensitive movement

16. John Hesselink, "Toward a Seminary That Is Catholic, Evangelical, and Reformed," *Reformed Review* 27, no. 1 (Fall 1973): 103–11.

17. Zondervan Academic, "New Studies in Dogmatics—A New 15-Volume Series in Constructive Theology," *Koinōnia* (blog), November 12, 2012, http://www.koinonia blog.net/2012/11/nsd.html (emphasis added).

that it has come to represent, is a quintessential example of a "correlationist" approach to congregational ministry, while City Church of San Francisco is an example of a "catholic-Reformed" approach. For decades, Willow Creek church has been known for its "seeker-sensitive" programs, which meet seekers where they are: programs target common "felt needs" in the culture, for example, how to deal with conflict, or how to have a positive family life. Promoting the rhetoric of moving beyond the "traditional" church, Willow Creek reoriented the whole idea of "church" to correlate to these felt needs. And scores of churches have followed Willow's lead.

In 2007, Willow Creek completed a self-study to see the results of this approach. It turns out that its programs were not leading to spiritual growth—they were not making disciples. "We made a mistake," Hybels said.[18] By orienting their programs toward felt needs, they were unintentionally funding central tenets of MTD: that religion is about *me*, meeting *my* needs, and making *me* happy. Theology and doctrine matter more than they realized.

Contrast this with City Church of San Francisco, which also has a proven track record of outreach to the unchurched, and is a leader of a network of city-center church plants around the country. At City Church, worship is "seeker-comprehensible"—so technical terms are elegantly explained—but it is deeply catholic and Reformed. Weekly worship includes a proclamation of God's Word together with a celebration of the Lord's Supper, in the tradition of the early church and reformers such as Calvin who desired a weekly celebration of the Supper. Rather than trying to "catch up" with the pop culture around it in the strategy of Willow, City Church is unafraid to create its own culture—a culture celebrating creation, the arts, and service to those

---

18. Bill Hybels, http://revealnow.com/story.asp?storyid=49. Hybels's full passage indicates that even as he admits this mistake, his response to the problem is an individualistic one that does not appear to recover the centrality of the Triune God's action: "We made a mistake. . . . What we should have done when people crossed the line of faith and became Christians, we should have started telling people and teaching people that they have to take responsibility to become self feeders. We should have gotten people (and) taught people how to read their Bible between services (and) how to do the spiritual practices much more aggressively on their own." See Ed Stetzer, "Weeping for Willow's Disciples," *Christianity Today*, July 7, 2008, http://www.christianitytoday.com/edstetzer/2008/july/weeping-for-willows-disciples.html.

most vulnerable in the city. City Church is mission-oriented, but in a way that sees God's work through Word and Sacrament as central to this mission. Its goal is not just to "get people saved," but to *make disciples*—thus there are numerous opportunities for laypeople to learn about Scripture, doctrine, and the life of prayer, developing their leadership skills for the congregation and the workplace. City Church is "traditional"—with a Sunday liturgy reflecting its catholic and Reformed theology. But it is not "traditional" in a 1950s, Midwest sense of the term. It is a distinctly Reformed church that seeks to draw upon the larger catholic tradition of theology and practice, for the sake of its mission and witness in the world. The felt needs of the culture do not drive its agenda. Its vision of the action of the Triune God in and through worship, fellowship, and service drives its agenda.

From this example, and by what I have said above, it should be clear that congregational ministry is a central site for the rediscovery of the catholic-Reformed tradition. It is not simply, or even primarily, a scholarly task. This is because of a particular theological conviction: the ministry of Word and Sacrament is a central site for God's activity in, through, and to the world. Stated in terms of the "missional church" movement—but in *contrast* to many contemporary visions of the "missional church"—Word and Sacrament are recognized as the central means by which God carries forward his "mission" to the world. Today's church needs pastor-theologians who are willing to dig deep into the biblical insights of the catholic and Reformed treasury of teaching and practices, rather than being guided by the latest whims or trends.

Nevertheless, there *is* a significant—and complex—scholarly task for rediscovering the catholic-Reformed tradition today. In the few pages that remain, I will "name" some of the movements with which catholic-Reformed scholars need to be engaged in pursuing the vision that I have outlined.

1. *Theological Interpretation of Scripture (TIS) and History of Biblical Interpretation.* This movement is essential for overcoming the archaeological and primitivist approaches to Scripture outlined above. In drawing upon the history of exegesis in a trinitarian, Christ-centered way, TIS engages in "post-biblical retrieval" of patristic,

medieval, and Reformation-era approaches to Scripture. But we must also remember that for the catholic-Reformed tradition, God's Word in Scripture always stands above the church and its post-biblical tradition; the living Lord of the church speaks through Scripture to promise, rebuke, assure, and guide his people. In addition, as I see it, the TIS movement is not "against" historical-critical approaches to the Bible; yet on their own, historical critical approaches are not sufficient for interpreting the Bible *as* Scripture. In the words of New Testament scholar Joel Green: "Any and all methods must be tamed in relation to the theological aims of Scripture and the ecclesial context within which the Bible is read as Scripture."[19]

2. *Movements Overcoming False Polarities in Describing Patristic and Reformation-Era Theology.* It is still popular for systematic theologians to make sharp polarities between the trinitarian theology of the East (Cappadocians) and the West (Augustine), as well as between the theology of Calvin and that of later "Calvinists" or scholastics.[20] There are genuine differences and contrasts, of course. But careful contextual historical work over the course of several decades of scholarship has shown that the common *sharp* polarities are based upon gross, non-contextual caricatures of Augustine and Reformed Scholasticism respectively. In my scholarly career, I have been amazed at how this in-depth historical work has been ignored by many theologians today,

---

19. Joel B. Green, *Seized by Truth: Reading the Bible as Scripture* (Nashville: Abingdon, 2007), 125.

20. These are, indeed, two distinct movements among historians of theology. But I pair them together because they share numerous historiographic assumptions, particularly in the way that they overcome false polarities (between Augustine and the Cappadocians, and between Calvin and the Calvinists) in favor of contextual historical accounts that undermine the convenient polarities of recent systematic theologians. Key scholars on the reassessment of the patristic sources are Lewis Ayres, Michel Barnes, Sarah Coakley, and Khaled Anatolios. Key scholars on the reassessment of Reformation and post-Reformation sources are David Steinmetz, Richard Muller, Timothy Wengert, Carl Trueman, and John L. Thompson. For further analysis of the historiographic assumptions involved, see Michel R. Barnes, "Augustine in Contemporary Trinitarian Theology," *Theological Studies* 56, no. 2 (June 1995): 237–50; J. Todd Billings, "The Contemporary Reception of Luther and Calvin's Doctrine of Union with Christ: Mapping a Biblical, Catholic, and Reformational Motif," in *Calvin and Luther: The Continuing Relationship*, ed. R. Ward Holder (Göttingen: Vandenhoeck & Ruprecht, 2013), 158–75; and J. Todd Billings, "The Catholic Calvin," *Pro Ecclesia* 20, no. 2 (Spring 2011): 120–34.

who have offered no substantial textual response on either account. In the words of David Bentley Hart:

> The notion that, from the patristic period to the present, the Trinitarian theologies of the Eastern and Western catholic traditions have obeyed contrary logics and have in consequence arrived at conclusions inimical each to the other—a particularly tedious, persistent, and pernicious falsehood—will no doubt one day fade away from want of documentary evidence. At present, however, it serves too many interests for theological scholarship to dispense with it too casually.[21]

Likewise, in spite of a vast amount of historical documentation to the contrary, the "Calvin versus the Calvinist" thesis remains a widespread assumption among theologians, because it is seen as theologically useful.[22] But in my view, it represents a tragic loss of an opportunity: for embracing recent contextually sensitive accounts can open up numerous creative and new opportunities for retrieval, reflection, and reconstrual of the tradition. In addition, these historical reassessments are important for a catholic-Reformed vision because they respond to the common caricatures of classical catholic theological positions, as well as classically Reformed ones—caricatures still fill the pages of many books (including textbooks!) today.[23] The point here is not about whether one "likes" Augustine or the Reformed scholastics. The point is first and foremost a descriptive one—that since these contextual accounts have broken through the common caricatures, theologians need to start telling a different historical story about these figures and movements.

3. *Non-Reformed Theologies of Premodern Retrieval.* These approaches generally share the goal with a catholic-Reformed approach of using premodern retrieval as a way to expose and destabilize our modern cultural captivities. They come in diverse forms. Often they occur *in response* to modern theologians of various "correlationist" orientations, such as Paul Tillich, Gordon Kaufmann, Sallie McFague, or James Cone. Here is a short list of these approaches: Roman Catholic

---

21. "The Mirror of the Infinite: Gregory of Nyssa on the *Vestigia trinitatis*," *Modern Theology* 18, no. 4 (October 2002): 541.
22. See Billings, "Catholic Calvin."
23. See the examples in Billings, "Catholic Calvin."

retrievals, Orthodox retrievals, Radical Orthodoxy, the "new Black theology" (Jennings, Carter, and others),[24] feminist retrieval theologians (Coakley, Tanner, and others),[25] and African theologies of retrieval (Bediako, Oden).[26] All of these provide points of difference, yet also areas for very fruitful dialogue and engagement with the catholic-Reformed tradition. For example, one contemporary Roman Catholic theologian of retrieval from whom I have benefited greatly is Matthew Levering. His work is not only useful in deepening our sense of the depth and viability of the premodern catholic tradition, but it has sharpened my appreciation of the Reformed tradition in particular. As a Roman Catholic Augustinian, Levering's theological vision illuminates the issues of divine agency, sovereignty, and election, for example, in a way that shares much with classical Reformed voices.

Of course, catholic-Reformed theologians should be in appreciative and critical dialogue with other movements as well, ones that I cannot pursue in this brief essay: the contemporary renewal in Barth studies, social and cultural history as a supplement to the history of theology, the theologies of the global South, and aspects of the missional church movement, to name a few. But these three areas above are especially key for developing a robust practice of *theological retrieval* as an alternative to correlationist approaches.

In the end, what is at stake in pursuing biblical, Christ-centered renewal along a catholic-Reformed path of retrieval? Nothing less than a reality at the heart of the Christian faith. In the words of the apostle Paul: "I have been crucified with Christ. It is no longer I who live, but Christ who lives in me. And the life I now live in the flesh I live by faith in the Son of God, who loved me and gave himself for

24. For an excellent short overview of this movement see Jonathan Tran, "The New Black Theology: Retrieving Ancient Sources to Challenge Racism," *The Christian Century*, January 26, 2012, http://www.christiancentury.org/article/2012-01/new-black-theology.

25. See especially Sarah Coakley, *God, Sexuality, and the Self: An Essay "On the Trinity"* (Cambridge: Cambridge University Press, 2013); Kathryn Tanner, *Jesus, Humanity, and the Trinity: A Brief Systematic Theology* (Minneapolis: Fortress: 2001).

26. See especially Kwame Bediako, *Theology and Identity: The Impact of Culture upon Christian Thought in the Second Century and in Modern Africa* (Eugene, OR: Wipf & Stock, 2011); Thomas Oden, *How Africa Shaped the Christian Mind: Rediscovering the African Seedbed of Western Christianity* (Downers Grove, IL: InterVarsity, 2010).

me" (Gal. 2:20). In the deeply countercultural words of the Heidelberg Catechism, "I am not my own, but belong . . . to my faithful Savior, Jesus Christ." We live in a consumerist, tinkering, MTD culture that is endlessly preoccupied with the self, its own needs, its own rights, and its own attempts to stand *above* history and tradition. It is a restless age, and Augustine was right in praying, "You have made us for yourself, Lord, and our hearts are restless until they rest in you."[27] The good news of the gospel is that we are not left to the restless, barren, MTD world in which we are the center. By the Spirit, we are *displaced*—we enter into a new drama, embrace a new identity—one in which we call God "Abba! Father!" (Rom. 8:31) as we find our life *in Christ*—Christ who lives in us by faith. Let us not settle for the "halfway good news," which is correlated with and accommodated to our own cultural captivities. Let us recognize that our true identity is this: we have been crucified with Christ, and we are not our own; our true life is found in him. For our only comfort in life and in death is that we belong—body and soul, in life and in death—to our faithful Savior, Jesus Christ.

27. Augustine, *Confessions*, trans. Henry Chadwick (New York: Oxford University Press, 2009), 3 (1.1).

Index